Drama Worlds

The Dimensions of Drama Series
edited by Cecily O'Neill

Drama for Learning by Dorothy Heathcote and Gavin Bolton

Drama Worlds by Cecily O'Neill

....

Drama Worlds
A Framework
for Process Drama

Cecily O'Neill

Heinemann

Portsmouth, NH

Heinemann

361 Hanover Street
Portsmouth, NH 03801-3912

Offices and agents throughout the world

Editor: Lisa Barnett
Cover art: Emily Berg/The Fringe

Excerpt from *Enter Talking* by Joan Rivers. Copyright © 1986 by Joan Rivers. Used by permission of Dell Books, a division of Bantam Doubleday Dell Publishing Group, Inc.

Excerpt from "Imaginary Gardens with Real Toads: Reading and Drama in Education" by
David Booth. Reprinted from *Theory into Practice* 24 (3) by permission of The Ohio State University and the author.

Excerpt from "Creating Multiple Worlds: Drama, Language and Literary Response" by
T. Rogers and C. O'Neill. Reprinted from *Exploring Texts: The Role of Discussion and Writing
in the Teaching and Learning of Literature,* edited by G. Newell and R.K. Durst. Copyright ©
1993. Reprinted by permission of Christopher-Gordon Publishers.

Library of Congress Cataloging-in-Publication Data
O'Neill, Cecily.
    Drama worlds: a framework for process drama/Cecily O'Neill
        p. cm. —(The Dimensions of drama)
    Includes bibliographical references and index.
    ISBN 0-435-08671-5
    1. Improvisation (Acting)   I. Title.   II. Series.
PN2071.I5053   1995   95-8111
792'. 028—dc20   CIP

Printed in the United States of America on acid-free paper

Docutech EB 2008

Contents

Prologue:
An Extended Process Drama

FRANK MILLER

There was a tense atmosphere in the circle of chairs. Each of those present had received an urgent message. The leader glanced around.

"I hope no one saw you come here. I sent for you because I thought you ought to know about it as soon as possible, since this affects us all. We are all involved. I received this note today. It says that Frank Miller is coming back to town."

A silence followed this announcement. Then the townspeople began to ask questions. When did the note arrive? How was it delivered? Was it signed? What did it mean? The leader told them that it had been found that morning, pushed under the front door. It was unsigned. It meant what it said—that after all these years, Frank Miller was coming back.

One person asked if Frank had been let out. No one knew. Why would he want to come back to the town after all these years? The leader said, significantly, that perhaps Frank had some unfinished business in the town and reminded everyone once again that this concerned them all. One person couldn't see why they should worry. Others, reminding her of what Frank used to be like, admitted that they were very worried.

Another person thought that maybe the note was just a joke. "Who would play such a cruel trick?" asked the leader. "Frank Miller," answered several voices. One of the townspeople suggested that maybe Frank himself had delivered the note. That meant he was already in town. After ten years he wouldn't necessarily be easily recognizable. Someone said, "He could be out there now, waiting for us." Everyone wondered what they should do. The leader stood up. "Well, that's up to you to decide. I just thought that since we were all involved ten years ago when we got rid of him, you had a right to know.

What you do about it is your business. I know what I'm going to do, I'm going to watch out for myself. You can do whatever you want. I think you'd better go now. And be careful."

This was the first episode of an extended improvisation session with high school students in Toronto. After the improvisation ceased, we talked out of role. What kind of place were we in? What period of history was this? Why were we so afraid of Frank Miller? What had we done to him ten years before, and why?

The students decided that the place was a small western town at the turn of the century. For some reason, the townspeople had hated and feared Frank, and ten years previously they had framed him, so that he was sent to prison. No details of how or why he had been framed were decided. The students were happy to let these facts emerge if we needed them.

In the next episode, we worked in small groups. The task was to discover what Frank Miller had been like in the past. Each group was asked to create a tableau, a frozen picture, showing a glimpse of Frank at different points of his life, from infancy to young manhood. We saw in succession a loner, an isolate, an alienated teenager who began to exert power over those around him through intimidation and violence, a young man who treated his friends and girlfriends with either brutality or indifference.

The next task was to discover whether Frank was already in town. Everyone tried to recall any strangers whom they might have seen in town. Where would such strangers be likely to go? Several people had been noticed around town—at the livery stables, the post office and the saloon. In small groups, we improvised encounters with some of these strangers as they went about their business—at the bank, the post office and the railway station.

It emerged that two strangers had been seen at the saloon, and either one of them could be Frank. Two of the boys became the strangers and sat with their feet up on the hitching rail (two chairs) outside the saloon. A girl took on the role of the sheriff. The group watched as she began to question the strangers. Where had they come from? Was this their first time in town? What were they doing here? One of the strangers was very affable and forthcoming; the other remained silent and brooding, and gradually the attention of the group became focused on him. The sheriff asked each of them his occupation. The first said he was a farmhand looking for work. The second said one word—"Hate." We had found Frank Miller.

Working in pairs, one student became someone in the town who had particular reason to fear Frank's return. The other took on the role of a friend to whom they confided their anxieties. Afterward, the confidantes met to discuss what they had heard, while their partners listened. It appeared that there were many people who either had a part in framing Frank or were likely to be the focus of his revenge. We learned a great deal about both Frank and his relationship to the community. The students decided that one person in particular was likely to be the focus of his hate. This was the postmistress, Sarah, who had been involved with Frank before he went away. She had somewhat of a reputation in the town. It appeared that she had been pregnant when he left town and now had a ten-year-old son. She had told her son that his father was dead.

At this point, the class took a break. When the students returned, there was a need to recapture the tension of the previous encounters. We played the game of Hunter and Hunted, and students took turns being either Frank, the Hunter, seeking his prey blindfolded, or Sarah, the Hunted, also blindfolded, trying to escape his clutches. The "feeling" quality of the game paralleled the developing theme of the drama.

Next, I narrated the story as it had developed up to this point to check for consensus and to give the students the opportunity to clarify details. The students decided that the next scene they wanted to explore was a meeting between Frank and his son. This would take place in the livery stables where the boy worked after school. Frank's purpose would be to discover as much as possible about the boy's home life, his relationship with his mother, and what he had been told about his father. They worked in pairs, one playing Frank and the other his son, and explored an encounter in which one of the characters had a precise but unstated purpose. In one of these pairs, it emerged that the boy had innocently invited Frank home for supper the next evening to meet his mother. The group agreed that this meal would be an interesting dramatic encounter to explore.

First, the boy had to tell his mother about his meeting with Frank. We set this up as Forum Theatre, and volunteers took on the roles of Sarah and her son. If they needed help, we could offer them dialogue or suggestions, and if we felt they needed to add anything to the scene, we could "freeze" the scene and give them our ideas. Both the actors and the observers had the power to stop the action scene at any moment and ask for help or offer dialogue or other advice. Once again, in this episode there was one innocent party and one with past knowledge upon which to draw and very differing expectations about the immediate future. The tension in both the observers and performers was considerable as we watched to see when and how Sarah would choose to tell her son the truth about his father.

For the next scene, the class was divided into three groups. Choosing to focus either on Frank, Sarah, or the boy, each group devised a dream sequence, which showed what their character, in this new situation, most wished or feared. These dreams were rehearsed and shared with the rest of the class and had all the nonnaturalistic features of a dream, including repetition, distortion, and extreme contrast of movement and words. Frank's fantasy was of a happy home life counterpointed with his dread of prison. The boy's dream showed his close relationship with his mother but his longing for a real father, and Sarah's nightmare was full of her distorted and exaggerated memories of Frank's true nature.

Next, the class worked in groups of three, as the mother, father, and son. In their own time, and without anyone's watching, they improvised the supper at which Frank and Sarah met for the first time after ten years. This was a tense scene, with Frank behaving in an ambiguous manner, Sarah trying to understand his real purposes, and the boy confused and anxious.

Because of the importance of this encounter, the group asked if they could watch it being reenacted. Three of the students volunteered to take on the roles of Frank, Sarah, and their son, and improvised the supper scene once again. Before the scene began we decided on the features of the room in which the meal took place and discussed what each of the characters might be feeling. Each character in the scene would have a different intention and bring different expectations to the scene. The truth of the situation began to emerge as the boy wondered at his mother's guarded and fearful reaction to Frank, and Frank's resentment of Sarah became more obvious. The tension between the burden of the past carried by Frank and Sarah and their fears and hopes for the future drove the scene forward. As it became clear that Sarah did not want Frank to be part of her life, the boy began to suspect that they were hiding something from him.

The scene grew more complex. Two more volunteers were chosen to take on the roles of Sarah's and Frank's inner voices. Now, as well as the dialogue spoken by Frank and Sarah, we heard their thoughts spoken aloud. The atmosphere became more intense as the characters' inability to convey their feelings became more obvious. Finally, Frank, in frustration and despair, pushed the table aside and raised his hand to strike Sarah. The boy rushed between them, and Frank's fist caught him. He ran from the house. Sarah and Frank were left looking helplessly after him, each more alone than ever.

In the final episode, the earlier tableaux were recalled, and the Frank figure in each one was asked to recreate his pose. These Franks arranged themselves in chronological order, with the final figure of Frank, reaching out for his son, his hope for the future, as the last figure in the sequence. We saw the progression of Frank Miller once again, from childhood to the loss of all of his hopes. The sequence was complete.

In this extended "process drama," it is possible to see a dramatic world come into being, an imagined elsewhere with its own characters, locations, and concerns, developing in accordance with its own inner logic. This world manifests tension and complexity, and employs devices similar to those appropriate to dramatic worlds arising in more conventional theatre settings. It is apparent that all those involved in *Frank Miller* were caught up in a dramatic experience that they created and maintained, yet which possessed no prior script, fixed scenario, or separate audience.

This process drama generated a text in action, appropriated the space in which it occurred, required the participants to project into a number of roles, and moved toward an unknown horizon of possibilities. Its duration of almost three hours allowed the pressures of the past as well as complex expectations about the future to develop in a dramatic present including elements of composition, spontaneous encounters, and group contemplation. The experience was its own destination and the group an audience to its own acts.

In this book, I hope to show that, when the imagined worlds of process drama develop an internal coherence and are appreciated for the same insights and purposes that are valued in any piece of theatre, participants experience a satisfying and significant dramatic encounter. I will explore the relationship between process drama and improvisation in theatre and trace some of the key elements in dramatic structure that are necessary components of the event.

Introduction

Process drama is a complex dramatic encounter. Like other theatre events, it evokes an immediate dramatic world bounded in space and time, a world that depends on the consensus of all those present for its existence. Process drama proceeds without a script, its outcome is unpredictable, it lacks a separate audience, and the experience is impossible to replicate exactly. But, I believe that it gives access to authentic dramatic experience for the participants and can be regarded as a legitimate part of the realm of theatre. Process drama shares the key features of every theatre event and is articulated through the same kinds of dramatic organization.

More than a decade ago, in *Drama Structures: A Practical Handbook for Teachers,* my co-author Alan Lambert and I attempted to provide teachers with a flexible framework to support their explorations in drama.

> If pupils are to grasp concepts, understand complex issues, solve problems and work creatively and cooperatively in drama, they will be helped by a clearly established context and a strong but flexible framework to support and extend the meaning of the work.[1]

The book is specifically aimed at drama teachers and makes close connections with a range of curricular material, including history, social studies, and literature, but the experience of the drama is also valued for its own sake. The significance of theatre elements such as tension and contrast within these drama structures is acknowledged, but it was not part of our purpose to explore their operation in any detail. In recent years I have come to realize that when the drama structures in this book give rise to a satisfying dramatic experience for the participants, it is not necessarily because of their explicit association with specific educational or theatrical purposes. They are most effective when they obey the intrinsic rules of a dramatic event.

···

Drama Structures is one of several publications that have helped teachers to moderate the unpredictability of improvisation by structuring and developing the dramatic encounter through a sequence of episodes. My purpose in this book is rather different. I hope to clarify the relationship between what I call process drama and the basic characteristics of the theatre event. Although it is generally accepted by drama teachers that their work observes the same rules and shares many of the features of theatre, the nature and application of these rules and attributes has not been closely investigated. This book examines the sources of process drama in effective "pre-texts," its connections with more familiar kinds of improvisation, the texts it generates in action, the kinds of role available to the participants, the operation of such factors as audience and dramatic time, and the significance of the leader's function in the event. Examples of the operation of these elements in a number of process dramas are provided, and particular dramatic strategies and characteristics are identified. The associations between theatre form and process drama are highlighted, and these explicit links should help to make the value of process drama more readily understood and appreciated, particularly by those working in actor training and theatre. The close affinities and connections that emerge between theatre and process drama may encourage theatre teachers and directors to explore this powerful and adaptable medium for their own purposes.

Process drama has the potential to engage participants in a search for dramatic significance through encountering and manipulating the fundamental features of the medium. Essential dramatic elements are managed by the leader and the participants in process drama so that it leads to both an authentic dramatic experience and a greater understanding of the nature of the event. Learning about drama occurs through engagement in the experience. Too often, theatre arts courses expose students' deficiencies and weaken their confidence by immediately requiring them to perform both formally and informally. For many, lack of experience and technique will make this a painful experience. Process drama, on the other hand, permits direct engagement with the event, a range of role taking, and an encounter with the power of drama without necessarily demanding the immediate display of sophisticated acting techniques.

Process Drama and Pre-texts

Throughout this book, I present two terms that may not be familiar to readers. The first is *process drama*, and I trace the development of this term in the next few pages. The notion of *pre-text* is one I have developed in recent years and found extremely useful for clarifying the means by which the drama world is set in motion. *Pre-text* refers to the source or impulse for the drama process, as I explain in Chapter 2. As well as indicating an excuse—a reason for the work—it also carries the meaning of a text that exists before the event.

Process drama is almost synonymous with the term *drama in education.* The phrase *process drama* seems to have arisen almost simultaneously in Australia and North America in the late 1980s as an attempt to distinguish this particular dramatic approach from less complex and ambitious improvised activities and to locate it in a wider dramatic and theatrical context. Dramatic activities in the classroom have been known as educational drama, classroom drama, informal drama, developmental drama, curriculum drama, improvisation, role drama, creative dramatics, and creative drama. Each of these labels is either limiting or tautologous. Although I believe the term *process drama* will be useful, the creation of a new label for this particular approach may not be the final answer to the problems of vocabulary that persist in the field.

In North America, the terms most commonly used to indicate exploratory dramatic activity where the emphasis is on process rather than on product are *creative dramatics* and *improvisation.* The latter term is less often used by British drama educators, perhaps because these teachers are concerned with establishing educational drama as a complex learning medium rather than an activity that can be seen as a mere rehearsal device, a display of skills without context or a brief entertainment. This is sometimes the way the activity is viewed in North America, where *improvisation* is almost synonymous with *skit* or *sketch.* Although Dorothy Heathcote, one of the pioneers of drama in education, referred to her work during the 1960s as *improvisation,* she uses the term very rarely in her later writings.

Process and Product

Process usually indicates an ongoing event, unlike *product,* a term that implies conclusion, completion, and a finished "object." A theatre piece is often regarded as a *product,* although it will be experienced by the audience as an event rather than as an art object. But every theatre event arises from a complex process of composition, rehearsal, and theatrical interpretation. Both *process* and *product* have the disadvantage of being simple terms required to indicate intricate structures. In improvised drama, process has been defined as "negotiating and renegotiating the elements of dramatic form, in terms of the context and purposes of the participants."[2] This definition could be applied with equal fitness to a process undertaken with a theatrical outcome in mind.

xvi   *Introduction*

. . . .

The term *process drama* usefully distinguishes the particular kind of complex improvised dramatic event, which is my subject in this book, from that designed to generate or culminate in a theatrical performance, but the difficulty is that it may suggest an opposition to product and perpetuate the sterile separation of this improvised approach from its dramatic roots. In fact, both process and product are part of the same domain. Like theatre, the primary purpose of process drama is to establish an imagined world, a dramatic "elsewhere" created by the participants as they discover, articulate, and sustain fictional roles and situations. As it unfolds, the process will contain powerful elements of composition and contemplation, but improvised encounters will remain at the heart of the event as the source of much of its dramatic power. Because improvisation is an essential component of the process, it will be important to consider the essential characteristics of this vital source of dramatic invention and discovery and trace the ways in which it has been used in rehearsal and performance, as well as to identify its significance in process drama.

The Characteristics of Process Drama

Process drama, like improvisation, proceeds without a written script but includes important episodes that will be composed and rehearsed rather than improvised. The essential difference between process drama and improvisation is that, as the term suggests, *process drama* is not limited to single, brief exercises or scenes. Instead, like any conventional theatre event, it is built up from a series of episodes or scenic units. This episodic organization instantly entails structure, because it implies a more complex relationship between parts of the work than the linear connections of sequence or narrative, where the segments of the work are strung together like beads on a chain rather than being part of a web of meaning.

The episodic structure of process drama allows the gradual articulation of a complex dramatic world and enables it to be extended and elaborated. As a result, it will take place over a longer timespan than most improvised activities. A further distinction is that brief improvisations typically involve only a few participants at a time, while the rest of the group provides an audience for their experiments. In process drama the entire group will be engaged in the same enterprise, and the teacher or leader may function within the experience as a playwright and participant. The work is not undertaken for any outside audience, but the participants are an audience to their own acts. I believe that the complexity indicated in this approach, involving an absence of script, an episodic structure, an extended timeframe, and an integral audience, is best indicated by the term *process drama.*

These features of process drama owe much to two of the most influential figures in drama in education, Gavin Bolton and Dorothy Heathcote. In *Towards a Theory of Drama in Education,* Bolton carefully articulated different modes of dramatic activity and showed how these modes could be combined to provide a satisfying and aesthetic experience for the participants.[3] The power and immediacy of Heathcote's work, her understanding of the operation of theatre elements within the improvised experience, the depth and significance of the contexts she chooses, and her work in role with the entire group have all been profoundly influential.[4] This book owes much to these outstanding artists and educators, although I have taken a different direction. My focus is specifically on the connections between process drama and theatre form; innovative theatre practice provides useful practical illustrations; explicit educational outcomes are less emphasized than the intrinsic dramatic fulfillment of the work; I rely heavily on the heritage of dramatic literature, and my examples are taken as much from the theatre as from education.

Process Drama and Contemporary Theatre

The evolution of process drama reflects developments in contemporary theatre, as well as being part of the creative and educational drama tradition. In the avant-garde theatre of the 1960s, the work of experimental practitioners and theorists emphasized notions of presence and immediacy, process and transformation, and these ideas filtered into the work of drama teachers in schools and colleges. More recently, influences from postmodern theatre practices are reflected in process drama. These include the fragmentation and distribution of roles among the group, a nonlinear and discontinuous approach to plot, the reworking of classic themes and texts, a blurring of the distinction between actors and audience, a double self-consciousness, and a constant shifting of perspectives.

The practices of drama in education, and by extension process drama, are increasingly recognized as radical and coherent theatrical experiences. They challenge traditional notions of the creation and function of character and narrative, as well as of a traditional spectator-performer relationship.[5] In what is one of the first uses of this term in print, Brad Haseman notes that those working in process drama have created, appropriated, and reshaped a range of dramatic forms that establish its unique character. For Haseman, these forms include role taking and role building, the "key strategy" of teacher in role, the means of being inside and outside the action, and distance and reflection.[6] In later chapters I will examine some of the sources of these "specific forms," their affinities with theatre heritage, theory, and practice and the ways in which they operate in process drama.

Owing to my emphasis on the dramatic and structural dimensions of process drama, examples will focus on the kinds of improvised approach that give rise to dramatic worlds rather than on those familiar activities whose purpose is to "warm up" the participants, create a sense of community, or enhance specific skills. However, even momentary exercises may have the power to evoke an imagined world. The fact that these worlds may be both brief and fragmentary need not invalidate them. Every work of art evokes an alternative world, even though this may not be explicitly structured in any ideal or complete way. Dramatic worlds generated in process drama are likely to be both impressionistic and fragmented but will still be capable of generating satisfactory experiences for the participants. Although these dramatic worlds develop spontaneously and in process, they possess their own structure, logic, and potential for growth. The embryo of process drama, like any other organism, carries within itself certain principles that constrain its development and suggest the specific features it may incorporate.

The extended and essentially improvisatory event that is process drama proceeds without a prewritten script, but an original "text" is always generated in action, and this text can be recalled and reflected on after the event. In theory it would be possible to construct a retrospective text of a process drama such as *Frank Miller* in even more detail than that provided at the beginning of this book. And, like a fragmentary play script, some elements of this experience may be reconstituted and repeated with another group.

Analyzing the Process

In suggesting ways in which process drama may be structured and organized, its immediacy and ephemerality must be respected. The process cannot be reduced to a series of predictable episodes or a fixed scenario. An effectively structured dramatic process will achieve development, articulation, and significance while avoiding the repetition of a carefully prearranged sequence, the transformation of process into superficial product, and the destruction of the spontaneity that is at the heart of the work.

Attempts to analyze any theatre event, however detailed, can never be more than tentative and partial. It is impossible to reconstruct the totality of any performance, but it is possible to grasp some of the basic organizing principles; and the same is true of even an essentially improvised event like process drama. A realistic attempt at structural investigation should ideally be a working analysis, indicating the ways in which the dramatic world has been constructed, and, particularly in the case of the complex improvised experience of process drama, pointing toward fruitful means of development and completion. In each chapter I provide a number of examples in which the operation of key dramatic elements in the structure are highlighted. These examples should be useful for those struggling to understand and implement the principles of this approach, and in theory they could be recreated with other groups. In no sense are they designed to provide scenarios to be reproduced exactly in other circumstances and on other occasions. They are meant to be descriptive and evocative rather than prescriptive, although readers may find them useful as pre-texts for their own explorations.

The Potential of Process Drama

Process drama functions with all the potentialities and limitations of the art form of drama. It offers a significant vehicle for prolonged and satisfying experimental encounters with the dramatic medium. While remaining apparently formless and undefined by a previous plan or script, it has a special capacity to lay bare the basic dramatic structures it shares with other kinds of theatre and that give it life. Satisfying experience in this approach can lead to a deeper understanding of drama itself and its essential underlying forms.

Various kinds of improvised activities have long been recognized in actor training and rehearsal as a means of cultivating the responsiveness and skill of the participants, but their capacity for developing a deeper understanding of dramatic purpose, form, and content has been largely unrecognized. The process of improvised drama is rarely sufficiently valued for its own sake, for the insights it can offer into the nature of theatre and performance, for the dramatic worlds it may generate, and for the significant encounters among participants that at its most articulate it can provide. The potential of process drama to provide actors in training and students of dramatic literature with a sound basis for understanding the medium of drama has still to be fully explored.

Actors, directors, and teachers who believe in the value of this process may encounter continual challenges in their work. Apart from pressures to turn an undervalued process into an overvalued product, the greatest obstacles are likely to be the problems of form and development arising from within the event. The best support for the efforts of those seeking to work in this exciting and experimental medium will come from a lucid and consistent understanding of the nature of process drama and its potential, a grasp of the conditions under which it is most likely to acquire a significant dramatic dimension, and a thorough knowledge of theatre form. Process drama is structured and developed in the same way that dramatic worlds occur in theatre, and participation in the creation of these worlds can be intrinsically satisfying, educationally worthwhile, and dramatically significant.

Encounters: Process Drama and Improvisation

■ **The purpose of engaging** in process drama is the same as that of encountering any of the other arts. Because it is active and collaborative, participants in process drama are required to think in and through the materials of the medium in which they are working and to manipulate and transform these materials. Process drama involves making, shaping, and appreciating a dramatic event, an experience that articulates experience. Participants control significant aspects of what is taking place; they simultaneously experience it and organize it; they evaluate what is happening and make connections with other experiences. These are all demanding activities, requiring the use of perception, imagination, speculation, and interpretation, as well as exercising dramatic, cognitive, and social capacities. These capacities and the energies of the group are focused on the development of a specific dramatic world arising from a particular pre-text that defines the parameters of this world.

Frank Miller, the process drama described in the Prologue, had as its starting point or pre-text the notion of a return, a common device in theatre form. Initially the leader is in control of several key elements, and in particular, the growth of the dramatic tension. The purpose of the pre-text, the return of Frank Miller, is to arouse anticipation in the group so that they begin to engage in and take responsibility for the development of the drama. An analysis of *Frank Miller* reveals the episodes or scenic units of which it is composed.

Episodes	Drama Elements
The leader in role speaks to the whole group and announces that news has come that Frank Miller intends to return to town. What is his purpose in coming back and	The **pre-text** immediately plunges the group into an imagined world, the details of which emerge as the participants contribute to the development of the scene.

what action should the towns-people take to protect themselves? There are implied questions about their involvement in Frank's departure ten years previously.	There is a strong sense of a shared past and anxiety about the future.
The leader clarifies some of the details that have emerged, and the group decides on further elaborations of time and place.	Negotiation **outside** the drama world, with conscious decisions about location and timeframe.
Working in small groups, the participants create tableaux of a number of moments in the early life of Frank Miller.	A **composed** activity, building the past and presented to the other participants as audience.
Improvised encounters. The students work in small groups as they meet and attempt to identify strangers at different locations in town.	These encounters occur simultaneously, and afterward the whole group **reflects** on the likely identity of each person encountered.
One of these encounters is recreated for the rest of the group, and it emerges that Frank Miller has indeed returned.	There is a strong sense of **audience** in this episode, and each spectator is working to interpret the meaning of the encounter.
Working in pairs, participants discuss the particular implications of Frank's return. What effect will it have on the lives of those who knew him well or feared him most? Half the group, the confidantes, reflect on the information acquired and share their fears for Sarah and her son.	Here, a more personal response to Frank's return is initiated. This work remains private, although later it is discussed in the larger group. It is here that the precise focus for the later work emerges.
Game—Hunter and Hunted. Two people are blindfolded, and one "hunts" the other within a circle of watchers.	This game reestablishes **tension** and recalls the feeling in the initial group meeting.
Narration by the leader to clarify the development of the work so far.	The participants assist in recalling details.

The students work in pairs. One is Frank and the other is his son. They meet for the first time.

This is a personal encounter, bringing deeper engagement in the role.

Forum Theatre. Two students volunteer to play the scene where Frank's child tells his mother about his meeting with Frank. By now, everyone has a stake in the outcome.

There is a strong sense of **audience** in this episode. It is possible for the spectators to suggest dialogue and reactions to the actors.

A Dream Sequence. The class works in three larger groups, creating a "dream" in sound and movement for either Frank, Sarah, or their son.

The same themes emerge powerfully in each "dream"—loss, longing, and the desire to belong.

In threes, the family has a meal. This is a naturalistic exploration, without previous rehearsal or preparation.

There is no audience to these explorations, although the leader monitors the development of the scenes.

Three volunteers recreate their scene for the rest of the group. Tensions grow between the characters. Inner "voices" are added. The scene ends with a threat of violence and the characters trapped in their own isolation.

Once again, there is a powerful sense of **audience** and considerable **tension**. There is an implicit sense of what the **future** may contain for the characters.

Earlier tableaux are recalled, and each of the Franks is isolated and placed in relationship to the others. One extra figure is added to the sequence to show Frank as he is at the end of the drama.

A timeline is created, recalling the development of Frank as an isolate in the community, and showing his struggles to transcend his circumstances.

The episodic and extended nature of this experience allows the participants to explore notions of belonging, of family and community relationships, of caring, of revenge, of absence and banishment, all from within the process. Each episode involves a different perspective on the event, permits an increasing level of personal and public engagement with the issues that emerge, and is based on an encounter of some kind. The event begins with the whole group and the leader in role, and this encounter immediately raises expectations about further encounters. Some scenes operate as dialogues, as in the meeting between Frank and his son. Each encounter contains a tension capable of driving it forward—the tension of a disguised identity, of a remembered past in meeting someone after many years; the tension of a hidden purpose, of a secret to be kept, of a position to be maintained—all operating within the larger tension of having to shut out what is actual and known in order to play the game of not knowing, illusion, and pretense.

In reflection, the students made both explicit and implicit connections with their own lives within the protection provided by the imagined context. I have found that however deliberately the drama may be distanced from real life, it is invariably the deepest concerns of their own lives that participants discover in the drama. The time, location, and characters of *Frank Miller* provide a perspective, an aesthetic distance from which the students are safe to confront community conflicts, family tensions, violence, and the absence or loss of a parent. As well as more personal connections, the students related their experience in the drama to plays and films they had seen and books they had read.

Using Process Drama

For the teacher or director, valid aims for any particular dramatic activity may include the illumination of some educational concern or a specific dramatic objective as well as the creation and exploration of a dramatic world for its own sake and the experience it affords the participants. In either case, if the process is allowed to grow in harmony with the rules of the dramatic medium, it will provide an authentic dramatic experience for the participants. In actor training or rehearsal, the purpose of the activity might be to reduce inhibition or to deepen characterization, and in education its aims might include motivating students to read or involving them in the investigation of historical, topical, or moral questions. In both theatre and education, improvised dramatic activities are most likely to be employed in the service of some extrinsic purpose, but the fact that the teacher or leader has a particular instrumental aim in mind will not necessarily preclude the growth of a dramatic world.

The materials of the school curriculum and the study of dramatic literature provide a potential source of significant content, but the dramatic dimension of this content will not necessarily be realized in the selection of forms of enactment. The symbolic or metaphoric aspects of the source or pre-text may be neglected, and there may be no sense of working in an artistic medium or within a dramatic tradition. When drama techniques are valued only for their capacity to promote specific competencies and achieve precise ends, and remain brief, fragmented, and tightly controlled by the teacher or director, the work is likely to fall far short of the kind of generative dramatic encounter available in process drama.

Process Drama and Literature

In the following example, the aim of the experience was to encourage ninth grade students to participate more directly in interpretation and reflection on literature. In the novel they were studying, *When the Legends Die,* a young Native American boy is taken from his environment and sent to a frontier school, where his identity is denied and his capacities overlooked.[1] The world evoked by the text is one of alienation and loss—the loss of family, habitat, culture, and identity. The challenge for the teacher is to give the students access to this remote and unfamiliar world through process drama and to empower them to address the issues in the novel with confidence in their own powers of judgement and appreciation.

The drama world came into being when the teacher in role as the principal of a frontier school welcomed the students as potential teachers to the school. The students questioned the principal and began almost immediately to challenge her view of the need to civilize and convert the Native Americans. In reflecting on this encounter, they connected the condescension and prejudice shown by the principal with attitudes they had experienced in their own school lives.

Next they were invited to work in pairs, either as a prospective teacher or as one of the Native Americans at the school. The students' view of their "education" began to emerge. Several students began to develop considerable commitment to their roleplay as Native Americans. They exhibited this commitment when once again they met with the principal. There was increasing criticism of the policy of the school and the attitude of the principal and empathy for the plight of the Native Americans. Suddenly, the discussion was interrupted by a student who began to role-play with a new level of engagement. What follows is a transcription of part of this interaction:

STUDENT: You took our homes. You expect us to adapt to your ways; why don't you adapt to ours?. . .You tell us we have to change—to go your way.

TEACHER:	Are you expecting me to go to your lodges? To your mountains?
STUDENT:	This is our land. You came here; you stole it.
TEACHER:	I'm afraid I can't quite agree with that . . .We made treaties with your people.
STUDENT:	And broke them. Broke them. You lied. White men lied.
TEACHER:	I don't pretend to be a politician; I'm just a teacher. I'm doing the best I can in difficult circumstances.
STUDENTS:	*(joining in)* It was our world first. You never owned it. You took it away from us. We were here first.

The student involvement and initiative that grew from encountering this curricular material fulfilled the teacher's educational purposes, but at the same time, it achieved a great deal more. There was an interpenetration of the drama world generated in the classroom with the world of the original novel. The novel operated as a pre-text, enriching, controlling, and sustaining the students' explorations, including the writing in role that concluded this work.

One of the written tasks for the students was to produce a school report on Bear's Brother, the hero of the novel. Two students produced the following work:

Student: Thomas Black Bear   *Subject:* Basketry   Thomas is a pleasure to have in class. He usually listens, although I frequently find him gazing out the window, as if he is looking for something. He sets himself apart from the other students and makes no attempts to have conversations with anyone in the class. However, his work in the class is unlike anything I have seen before. He won't use the materials I give him, but uses willow stems instead. His fingers are extremely dextrous, and his work is of very high quality. I'm not sure about any of his other classes, but Tom has a born-in skill in basketweaving. His ability is uncanny, and his work is superior to mine.

English Interim Report: Bear's Brother (Thomas)   Thomas is a very disruptive child. He rarely pays any attention in class and spends all his time staring at a window. He insists the subjects taught here are of no use to him. He is also very reckless. He picks fights and interprets things the wrong way. He can't control his temper; he's like a savage who has no rules to live by. The school faculty has tried to discipline him, but unfortunately, our attempts have ended in failure. I don't know what to do.

Involvement in the drama has given these students a new perspective on the text. They have projected imaginatively into the attitudes of the teachers the young Native-American boy might have encountered. Writing in role allows them to display and extend their understandings of the issues in the novel.[2]

Strategies Outside the Process

It may not always be relevant to the teacher's purposes to develop a dramatic strategy intended to achieve a particular aim into an extended dramatic world. Working on Brecht's *Mother Courage and Her Children,* I asked graduate students at the Ohio State University to work in groups and choose a scene from the play in which public events were mentioned. The task was to present the events in the scene as television news items. Each group delivered the "news" in a typical television format, with news anchors, commentary from "experts," and interviews with both those directly involved and innocent bystanders. The advantages of this task were that it encouraged the students to look closely at the original text, to play with their understandings of the work, to use anachronistic conventions to achieve an appropriately Brechtian degree of distance, and to contribute a further level of ironic commentary on the public and private events of the play. The task was firmly focused on the world of the original script and designed to illuminate both the content and structure of the work. On this occasion, a parallel or alternate world was not expected to grow from the activity. Although the strategy of replaying dramatic events as a TV news item might easily be included in a process drama, my purposes here were different and more limited. The exercise was not designed to evoke a dramatic world with potential for further development, but to serve my more limited objectives for the class. Within this restricted purpose, the task proved to be both illuminating and worthwhile.

Dramatic explorations of curriculum materials that remain exercise-based, short term, teacher-initiated and -directed, and task-oriented, as in this example, can prove useful in spite of their limitations. But, when the emphasis remains firmly on the instrumental purposes of these activities with little recognition of further possibilities, there will be few opportunities for the growth of an imagined world. Where teachers overemphasize predetermined "learning areas" and themes of an obvious educational nature, much of the potential for exploration and discovery will be lost. The same difficulty can arise in theatre. Early critics of Ibsen, for example, emphasized the social protest features of his plays rather than considering their poetic or dramatic qualities. The issues in Ibsen's plays—pollution, women's rights, heredity—were seen as their most significant and characteristic element.

Opportunities for discussion, reflection, and understanding are all good reasons for using drama activities, but these efforts may fall short of achieving their full potential. This happens when teachers fail to recognize the importance of the dramatic nature of the undertaking, as well as the significance of the form in which the subject matter is articulated. Source material for drama may be chosen for its social or moral significance, and not necessarily for its suitability for imaginative transformation and dramatic exploration. Investigations of social issues—the destruction of the rain forest or the problems of the Third World, however important or topical in themselves—are unlikely to be easily transformed into effective pre-texts for the growth of a dramatic world. In exploring these issues teachers may employ drama strategies that are capable of evoking imagined worlds, but these worlds will not flourish if they are inhabited predominately for didactic purposes. Under these conditions the drama activities may still retain a potential dramatic dimension, but it will be almost impossible for this dimension to develop within the constraints of the teacher's prescriptive goals. However, even in such limiting circumstances, it is conceivable that the students may experience the excitement and potentiality of an active, collaborative means of processing and representing their understandings.

Improvisation in Actor Training and Rehearsal

Improvisation techniques in the theatre can be employed for specific and limited purposes, as in the examples given from drama in education, or may be used more organically, with a sound understanding of their deeper uses. Improvisation exercises in actor training and in rehearsal promote spontaneity and a sense of community as well as allowing actors to practice specific technical competencies. In spite of the limitations of time and purpose, there is no reason why many of the approaches used by innovative theatre teachers and directors should not be capable of evoking complex dramatic worlds and achieving similar rewards for the participants.

Many directors and theatre teachers use improvised activities ranging from basic physical and vocal exercises to explorations that may become the source for entire performances. Even at a basic level, games and exercises operate to "warm up" the actors; overcome difficult rehearsal conditions; establish the authority, style, and personality of the director; suppress the actors' inhibitions; encourage risk taking; and most important of all, generate a sense of collective identity and community. This group feeling and sense of common purpose fosters the energy that drives the rehearsal process forward. Improvised activities allow the actors to step aside from the pressures of the script and explore aspects of character and situation without being subject to the immediate discipline of the script. But this does not mean that improvisation is an easy option. Improvisation always exacts more from actors than remaining strictly within the limits of a scripted situation. For the director, setting up improvisations demands skill in establishing a structure that leaves the actors free to create, but at the same time focuses and supports their work and directs their attention.

As in education, improvised activities in theatre settings are often bound by limited instrumental purposes and regarded merely as preparatory exercises or as a means of elaborating roles and stage business. The potential of familiar improvisation exercises to evoke fruitful dramatic worlds or to be included within the more challenging mode of process drama needs to be clearly recognized by those working in actor training or rehearsal.

Our current understanding of improvisation owes a great deal to the influence of Stanislavski; it was a key element in his approach to the training of actors. Stanislavski sought to replace a conscious, mechanical, and long-established theatrical tradition with a creative process in which conscious and subconscious absorption and sincerity blended to produce inspiration. Among the means he proposed for actors in training were observation, imagination, concentration, relaxation, sense memory, and adaptation. These approaches, in which improvisation was central, were designed to remove obstacles to the actors' development and help them use their personal resources more effectively. This is the message of his most influential work, *An Actor Prepares.*

> Today we did a series of exercises, consisting of setting ourselves problems in action, such as writing a letter, tidying a room, looking for a lost object. These we framed in all sorts of exciting suppositions, and the object was to execute them under the circumstances we had created. To such exercises the Director attributes so much significance that he worked long and enthusiastically on them.[3]

Because these exercises require the actors to project into an imagined situation and develop "exciting suppositions," they have the potential to develop a life of their own and evoke dramatic worlds.

However, the focus remains on the skill of the actor and the training possibilities offered by the dramatic situation, the problem in action, rather than on its intrinsic potential as a dramatic event in its own right.

Some of the exercises or scenarios described by Stanislavski make compelling reading and seem to have been powerful experiences for those involved.

> We ... threw ourselves into the improvisation with every ounce of energy. We seemed actually to be in Maria's apartment and to believe that the former tenant, who had become violently insane, had sought refuge there; the problem of how he would try to escape capture became real; and when Vanya, who held the door shut, suddenly jumped away, we fled, the girls screaming with sincere terror.[4]

Here there is a real sense that a world is coming into being, a world in which lunatics invade one's apartment and have to be recaptured. But the emphasis is on a moment of intensity, and the purpose is to release the actors into feeling and representing that moment convincingly, rather than exploring the nature and limitations of this imagined world, the previous history of the mad tenant, his purposes in returning to the apartment, his relationship with Maria, or other possibilities.

Because an exercise is spontaneous will not necessarily mean that it is capable of generating a dramatic world. Peter Brook, who engages his actors in "hundreds of exercises for months and months" to obtain "absolute freedom and absolute discipline," set up the following technical exercise in rehearsal. The task for the actors was to communicate with others sitting in the balcony of the theatre or with the musicians. The purpose was to achieve "wholeness of volume" while avoiding the dangers of too much intimacy, essential if the audience is to see everything and hear everything. Although the task is improvised, an imagined world is very unlikely to arise from this kind of specialized vocal exercise.[5]

Rehearsing Genet's *The Balcony* with actors from very different backgrounds, Brook used long evenings of "very obscene brothel improvisations" to enable a diverse group of people to come together and find a way of responding directly to one another.[6] In fact, these explorations are likely to have achieved important outcomes other than the loosening of inhibitions and the creation of an ensemble. They launched the task of establishing the nightmare world of Genet's brothel, as well as informing and enriching the actual realization of the play on stage.

The British director Joan Littlewood prepared for a production of Brendan Behan's *The Quare Fellow* by making the world of the play tangible for the actors through improvisation. Rehearsals were well under way before the cast were given scripts or particular parts were allocated. Instead, the task for the actors was to create the atmosphere and routines of prison life in order to bring into being and make concrete the world of the play. They spent a great deal of time marching around and around the flat roof of the theatre as prisoners on exercise.

> The day to day routines were improvised, cleaning out cells, the quick smoke, the furtive conversation, trading tobacco and the boredom and meanness of prison life were evolved . . . when (the script) was finally introduced the situations and the relationships had been well explored.[7]

Where a dramatic world begins to grow from improvisation in rehearsal, another significant function emerges. If the director skillfully sets up situations for the actors to explore and provides a secure framework for the improvised activities, a deeper understanding of the world of the play begins to emerge. Embedded within improvisations of this kind and waiting to be brought into conscious awareness lies what Marowitz calls the "theatrical syntax" on which the production will eventually be constructed.

When a director uses improvisation in rehearsal so that a parallel dramatic world is encouraged to grow, it can powerfully illuminate the original text. Rehearsing *Measure for Measure,* Charles Marowitz began by creating a trial scene at which all of the characters from the play were called on to give testimony, the subject of the hearing being the alleged violation of Isabella by Angelo. This improvised judicial inquiry made the actors aware in a clear, existential way of the details of the play and gave them the first budding awareness of what they, as characters, might feel about it. The improvisation involved discovery for the actors and was a diagnostic tool for the director who could first identify the actors' responses and then bring these responses into awareness.[8]

Here the relationship of the actors to the original playtext has been redefined. It has become a pre-text for the growth of an alternative dramatic world, but one that parallels and echoes the essential concern of the play with justice, judgement, and forgiveness. There is a dynamic tension between the characters as they exist and operate in the original text and the responses of the actors/characters in this improvised extension of the imagined world of the play. It is interesting, and somewhat unusual, that Marowitz sees the director as essential in the process of growth toward the actors' achievement of insight and awareness. Many directors using improvisation in rehearsal prefer to remain at the edge of the action, providing activities and suggesting ideas, side-coaching and commenting on the results.

The most effective rehearsals are those where the strongest experiences are provoked in the actors so that the living material of their roles and situations can be existentially explored. It is only through the actors that any experience is conveyed to an audience, and unless they have created their own experience in rehearsal, there is literally nothing to be conveyed.

Extended Explorations

In the preceding examples, time is a significant factor. Stanislavski, Brook, and Littlewood all encouraged their actors in extended exploration, unconstrained by the pressure to present their explorations to an external audience or to focus on technical mastery. It appears that these explorations were usually developed in response to external suggestions from the director rather than articulated in a sequence of episodes with a range of styles, as in process drama. The emphasis was on understanding and articulating the world of the play, on exploring character and setting, and these discoveries eventually had their outcome in performance.

Even when dramatic activities in the classroom and the rehearsal studio are intended primarily to achieve particular ends, they may still effectively transcend narrow instrumental confines. In the realm of theatre, the creation of dramatic worlds is the purpose of the enterprise. Here, at least in theory, improvised activities have the potential to develop a life of their own when they develop beyond the level of exercise, game, or training and when dramatic worlds are encouraged to grow in accordance with the rules of the medium. When the work transcends didactic or technical purposes and achieves a satisfying sense of form and coherence, while retaining the genuine immediacy, spontaneity, ingenuity, and playfulness that are among its essential characteristics, it will indeed be a genuine process.

It may be useful at this point to recall the features of process drama that I identified earlier. The key characteristics of process drama include the following:

- Its purpose is to generate a dramatic "elsewhere," a fictional world, which will be inhabited for the insights, interpretations, and understandings it may yield.

- It does not proceed from a prewritten script or scenario, but is likely to be based on a powerful pre-text.
- It is built up from a series of episodes, both improvised and composed or rehearsed.
- It takes place, therefore, over a timespan that allows this kind of elaboration.
- It involves the whole group in the same enterprise.
- There is no external audience to the event, but participants are audience to their own acts.

Although the work may take place in the context of the rehearsal studio or the classroom and serve specific purposes for the director or teacher, if it is successful, it will never be entirely bound by those purposes. Engaging in the range of complex and challenging activities that make up process drama may throw light on a particular theme or issue, extend knowledge of particular dramatic or literary texts, highlight specific theatrical forms, and exercise individual competencies, but it possesses the potential to go beyond these outcomes. Like theatre, it is possible for process drama at its best to provide a sustained, intensive, and profoundly satisfying encounter with the dramatic medium and for participants to apprehend the world in a different way because of this encounter.

From the moment of its inception, the spontaneity of process drama is supported, contained, and articulated by the embryo at its core—its inherent dramatic structure. When process drama develops in harmony with the principles of theatre form, when an understanding of dramatic structure gives unity and coherence to the work, and when the spontaneous experience is not subverted by pressures of audience, end-product, or limited instrumental demands, it becomes possible for it to evolve into a significant dramatic event, as immediate, engaging, and necessary as the best of any other kind of theatre.

Designs for Action: Scripts and Texts

■ **The growth of dramatic** worlds through improvised activities is inevitably restricted when these worlds are used for limited instrumental purposes. Another kind of constraint operates when performance is the intended outcome of the work. Throughout the history of the theatre and in many different cultures, improvisation has been used to create a huge variety of performance events. Nowadays, the most familiar and accepted form of improvised performance in our culture is probably that created by comedy improvisation ensembles like Chicago's Second City group. These ensembles often use suggestions from the audience as starting points, and the emphasis is always on entertainment. But even with the pressures operating in these settings, it is possible for a dramatic world with its own logic and development to come into being on stage.

I have used the comedienne Joan Rivers' account of working at Second City to examine an improvised comic episode for its essential dramatic elements.[1]

Improvisation	Drama Elements
One night, during the intermission, somebody called out "farmer and a hooker" as an improv request. Upstairs in the dim room, my heart pounding, I marched up to Bill Alton and said, "Let's you be the farmer and I'll be the hooker." To my amazement, he smiled and said, "Okay, I'll be coming to your room."	The audience provides the starting point for the work, the **pre-text**. At first the actors are inventing consciously, casting the roles and deciding the **setting**. These roles are clichés, and the challenge to the actors is to be inventive and creative within these limits, without overstepping the bounds of decency.

Onstage, Bill spoke first, saying, hot and bothered, "I shouldn't be here. I'm a happily married man." I answered, without thinking, my fear suddenly gone, "Everybody has problems, mister. I understand. A lot of my customers are married men."

The farmer develops a sense of the **past**, a life outside this particular situation, but implicated in it.

"Yes," said Bill, handing the initiative back to me, "but I have two wonderful children."
"I have two also," I said. "Plus one on the way," patting my stomach.

The hooker also develops a **past** and the actors begin a kind of competition, each raising the stakes on the other. There is a kind of **status game** in progress.

In pantomime, he showed me pictures of his children. I had none, I told him, because my wallet had been stolen—but I had a tattoo on my thigh. "Actually, I like the tattoo better," I said. "If I flex my muscle I can make my kid dance."

The imaginary pictures and tattoos authenticate the characters' lives and increase the sense of **display** and **competition** that is often a feature of this kind of improvised event.

On and on we went, gently jousting—my mind going click, click, click—like doing a puzzle in a flash, knowing instantly where to extend the line to the next dot. I was astonished, electrified, relieved—absolutely thrilled. So *this* was improvising, and it was inside me. Now Bill was forcing the scene to some finish we had not yet imagined. He said, "Well, let's get started," and began unbuttoning his shirt. I said, "Fine," and just stood there—which threw him another curve.

At this point, the actors have transcended conscious invention, and are working intuitively, supported by their understanding of the nature of the work.

The scene must not be prolonged beyond a certain point. Some kind of **resolution** is required.

He said, "Aren't you going to get undressed? It's a hooker's job to get undressed."
Faster than thought, the ending popped out of my mouth. "I don't

A **surprise** ending overturns the audience's expectations, and yet is logical in terms of the initial roles the audience has provided— "hooker" rather than "prostitute."

know what kind of women you deal with. I always stay dressed when I hook my rugs. Now, what do you want? A six by ten? An eight by eleven? We're having a special on throw rugs."

The actors have risen to the challenge, and won the contest.

The light, controlled backstage, blacked out. The audience booed delightedly.

The **conspiracy** with the audience is overturned and the event comes to a satisfying conclusion.

The two actors in this scene are working without a script and yet generating a valid dramatic experience. This experience uses a joke structure, status games, authentication, absurdity, display, competition, surprise, and reversal to achieve its effects. The actors are taking risks, as they embody possibility in feeling and imagination. Their resourcefulness and expertise creates improvisation that in Keith Johnstone's phrase is "additive rather than subtractive."[2] They generate a "text," one that did not exist prior to the event but which will persist in the memory of both performers and audience and is preserved and passed on in the telling, as well as in this published description. These skilled improvisers perform with the kind of spontaneity and imagination that have invigorated the theatre throughout its history. Such displays are usually regarded as mere entertainment, and although the skill of the performers is a source of delight to the audience, the instinctive understanding of the essence of the theatre event, which is the secret of their accomplishment, is overlooked.

Process drama shares the essential characteristics of immediacy, spontaneity, energy, and ingenuity with other kinds of improvisation. The most obvious feature of these events is that they develop without a written script. This absence of script or text has placed process drama, like most improvised dramatic activity, outside the generally accepted realm of theatre. The absence of a script and the difficulty of reliably recording and preserving improvised drama may explain why this exciting, unstable, and ephemeral form has been generally overlooked by academics and commentators. Although improvisation has been a powerful source of dramatic invention and discovery and an influence on dramatists through the ages, for some academics the word *improvisation* seems to signify everything objectionable in alternative forms of theatre.

Even that most influential of improvised theatre, the Commedia dell'Arte, is rejected by the critic Allardyce Nicoll, who claims that

the difference between the display of actors who have memorized
an author's lines and that of comedians inventing dialogue on the
spur of the moment must produce two entirely different impressions . . . as a result these two performances must be regarded as
wholly distinct in kind.[3]

Nicoll makes the questionable assumption that actors merely memo-
rize, transmit, and "display" the author's words and that improvisation will always be in the comic mode.

In conventional theatre the performance is always more than a
simple recreation of the script. The theatre event springs first from a
unique dynamic among the performers and then is realized in a further encounter between the performers and their audience, whether
or not the event has originated in a play script. At best, the script only
partially conserves the action, and every effective production of a
play will establish a unique style and rhythm as well as a distinctive
interpretation of the playwright's vision. The difficulties of analyzing
or recording even the most conventional theatre production lie in
this singularity and will not disappear merely because the event originates in a script.

The Text as Potential

Although the existence of the written script gave European drama its
status as an art form and a literary genre, its privileged position as
the primary meaning-maker in the event has been constantly challenged. The script is now recognized as only one sign system among
many, although it may continue to be a significant one. It represents
a stage potentiality, a written pre-text for the actual "performance
text" that is generated on stage. This performance text encompasses
all the aural, visual, gestural, and spatial elements of the actual performance, as well as the dynamics of the encounter between actors
and audience. The performance text is evidence after the fact of performance, as much a written record of what has taken place on stage
as a blueprint for reconstructing the theatre event.

If we are to understand the operation of text in improvisation, it
will be important to consider some of the different ways in which
texts may evolve, to examine the playwright function in the evolution
of these texts, and to determine the extent to which improvised texts
may be prearranged or recalled and repeated. Performance texts
may be developed from suggestions provided by the audience, as in
The Farmer and the Hooker example, from acting exercises, from the

actors' personal explorations, from encounters with existing texts, and, in process drama, from what I call pre-texts.

Weaving the Text

It is worth remembering that the word *text,* before it referred to a written or spoken, printed or manuscript text, meant a "weaving to-gether." In this sense it is clear that there can be no performance without text, but while there is always a text, there may not always be a written script. It is useful to conceive of the text, whether written, improvised, or transcribed, as the "weave" of the event. Instead of re-garding it as a linear set of directions, it is possible to perceive the text as a design for action, a kind of net or web woven tightly or loosely and organizing the materials of which it is made. It comes into being *during* the dramatic event. This will be particularly helpful in thinking about the text of process drama.

The dramatic text has been usefully defined as that which lends itself to a fiction, and is capable of being translated into a possible world.[4] Possible worlds will arise in conventional plays, in perfor-mances that are based on or consist entirely of improvisation, and in process drama. Process drama, whose nature is primarily defined by the absence of any prior literary document and which finds its mean-ing and being only in action, will generate a text made up of a similar network of relationships to those forged in any other theatre event. As I emphasized earlier, this text will evoke a possible world or pos-sess the potential to be translated into a possible world. There is, in effect, a "latent" text in every improvised drama. In theory it might be possible to record or transcribe this text, and like any conven-tional play script, it has the capacity to generate further dramatic events. The key question for the leader is how best to begin the weav-ing of the latent text of process drama.

Pre-texts

Although process drama may lack an obvious textual source, it will never arise in a vacuum. The dramatic world may be activated by a word, a gesture, a location, a story, an idea, an object, or an image, as well as by a character or a play script. I have found it useful to de-scribe these occasions for initiating dramatic action as *pre-texts.* It is the pre-text that will provide a firm base for the dramatic encounter of process drama.

An effective starting point will launch the dramatic world in such a way that the participants can identify their roles and responsibilities and begin to build the dramatic world together as rapidly as possible. Drama teachers and leaders are familiar with the notion of a "stimulus" as the source of the dramatic activity, but a pre-text is much more than this. The term *stimulus* has disagreeably mechanical overtones, rather than conveying an organic implication. A pre-text has a precise function that goes much further than merely suggesting an idea for dramatic exploration. The function of the pre-text is to activate the weaving of the text of the process drama. As well as indicating that it not only exists prior to the text but also relates to it, the term is valuable because it carries the further meaning of an excuse, a reason.

In process drama the pre-text operates, first of all, to define the nature and limits of the dramatic world and, second, to imply roles for the participants. Next, it switches on expectation and binds the group together in anticipation. The pre-text that is the source of the work is different from the text generated by the process, which remains as an outline, a trace, in the memories of the participants after the event. The latter is an outcome, a product.

Many of the suggested starting points in practical handbooks for leaders and teachers of improvised drama remain at the level of stimulus and never operate as pre-texts. Viola Spolin's influential book, *Improvisation for the Theatre*, provides familiar stimuli in the form of questions—what, where, who, why—directed at those about to begin an improvisation. These questions may promote ingenuity and inventiveness, but a mere accumulation of detail about character and situation will not necessarily function as an effective pre-text for action. In fact, they may burden the participants with information and motivation that will be impossible to access in a brief improvisation. The actors from Second City were given only their roles and built the encounter from that point through their own invention.

Pre-texts in Process Drama

An effective pre-text or preliminary frame for process drama will carry clearly accessible intentions for the roles it suggests—a will to be read, a task to be undertaken, a decision to be made, a puzzle to be solved, a wrong-doer to be discovered, a haunted house to be explored. A popular pre-text among drama teachers is the following announcement, from *Drama Structures:*

$100
offered to anyone willing
to spend one night in
DARKWOOD HOUSE

This announcement hints at the past and suggests the future, but within a firm dramatic present. It offers a task and implies roles for the participants. It operates functionally in a similar if much less complex way to Marcellus' question at the beginning of *Hamlet:* "What, has this thing appeared again tonight?" Here, Shakespeare economically informs us in a single line that it is nighttime, that a "thing" has appeared on a previous occasion, and that the characters fully expect it to show up again.

An illustration in a children's picture book, *Would You Rather?*, by the British author John Burningham was the source of the original idea for this pre-text. A little boy is shown sitting at the bottom of a staircase in a derelict house. The text asks: "Would you rather jump in the nettles for $5, swallow a dead frog for $20, or spend all night in a creepy house for $50?" This image provided the original impulse for *The Haunted House*.

Strategies	Drama Elements
The teacher introduces herself as Mrs. Brown, the owner of the house. The participants, a seventh grade class, are people who have seen the advertisement and are eager to accept its conditions. In response to their questions, she fills in some of the background—her attempts to sell the house, the fact that the local people are superstitious about it.	The advertisement, written on the blackboard, focuses the attention of the group, unites them in **anticipation**, validates the context, and begins the process of creating a dramatic world. Rather than explicating all the details of the house's history, the teacher responds to the students' questions but is evasive at times.
Working in pairs, one student takes on the role of a local person who knows all the stories that are told about the house, and the other remains in role as one of the people who plan to spend the night in the house.	The students create the **past** and the reasons for the sinister atmosphere connected with the house.
The students who have heard these stories now share them with each other. The "locals" listen to this retelling.	The stories are accepted as wild rumors about the house rather than as hard fact.

Further developments of this pre-text included interviews with people who might have access to real information about the house, for example the doctor, the oldest inhabitant, the minister, the police, the librarian. Students presented tableaux of the troubled history of the house and created documents that authenticated various incidents—a will, an obituary, newspaper articles, medical reports, the writings on the gravestones in the cemetery. On different occasions, different explanations for the house's sinister reputation were discovered. One group concluded that it was haunted by an uneasy ghost whose remains had to be found and given a decent burial before it could rest; on another occasion a class of third graders decided that Mrs. Brown had been cheated of her inheritance by the local doctor, who had killed her uncle and forged his will; ninth graders decided that Mrs. Brown had been cruelly treated in the house as a child, and that this was her way of banishing her fears; college students resolved the drama by announcing that all the local people were involved in a conspiracy, which involved kidnapping young women and turning them into surrogate mothers. For each group that works with this pre-text the drama develops in a different way and reaches a different conclusion.[5]

THE FUNCTION OF THE PRE-TEXT

The ideal pre-text "rings up the curtain" by framing the participants effectively and economically in a firm relationship to the potential action. It may hint at previous events and foreshadow future occurrences so that the participants develop expectations about the dramatic action. The pre-text will also determine the first moments of the action, establishing location, atmosphere, roles, and situations. It provides the arc from which it is possible to begin to infer the full circle of the action. The pre-text, and in some cases the first scene, episode, or interaction of a process drama, may be readily recalled or repeated by the participants or by the leader on another occasion. In this way a pre-text like *The Haunted House* may be explored a number of times by different groups, with many variations in its development and articulation. The pre-text will operate on these different occasions as a kind of "holding-form" for any meanings to be explored.[6] The effectiveness of the pre-text will depend in large measure on its essential simplicity, its minimal character, and its implications for action, and these are the qualities that will make it available for further use.

In setting up *Frank Miller,* the process drama described in the Prologue, I had a simple pre-text to guide me. This was the familiar dramatic idea of a *return,* in this case the return of someone to a small community after a period of years in order to complete some unfinished business. This return affects the lives of the whole community to a greater or lesser extent. This situation has been used by playwrights down through the ages, from the fatal return from Troy in Aeschylus' *Agamemnon* to Pinter's *The Homecoming,* where a son returns from America with his wife to the family home. My direct models were the return of Eilat Lovborg in *Hedda Gabler* and the release from prison of Frank Miller in the film *High Noon.* These pretexts supplied the notion of a community responsible for some slightly dubious or ill-advised past action. Immediately there is guilt and doubt and the threat of an outsider's arrival, a stranger who might seek revenge and whose return puts the stability of the community at risk.

The most important step for the leader in process drama is to find a starting point, an initial image, impulse, or interaction. The choice of pre-text will then initiate the essential process of selection that is necessary before a dramatic world can be evoked. It will establish the name of the game, and while offering certain possibilities, exclude others and provide built-in constraints. In children's play, pre-texts operate in very similar ways. "Cops and Robbers" is clearly a game offering different experiences and encounters from a game of "Doctors and Nurses." The pre-text furnishes an excuse for an immediate action or task or carries an implication of further action, so that the participants' anticipation and search for fulfillment can begin.

Playwright Function

In any text that develops from process drama or improvisation, a playwright *function* will always be present. This function may be in the hands of the dramatist, the director, or the ensemble, or it may be undertaken before our eyes by the actors. In process drama this playwright function is largely the responsibility of the teacher or leader, at least in the initial stages of the work. The leader may determine the choice of pre-text that will launch the dramatic world, and this immediately sets the parameters. In *The Haunted House,* a number of decisions were taken by the leader before the work began; for example, the kind of atmosphere that would be established and the essential problem with which the groups would be faced. The key to establishing the atmosphere of mystery was, paradoxically, to insist on the opposite. Mrs. Brown was cheerful and down to earth and continued to assert the normal character of the old house and the foolishness of believing in superstitions in this modern age. Later, as the work developed, this playwright function was shared among the participants. However it originates, the text of any improvised drama is clearly not a prior document, but a kind of *animating current* to which the actors submit.

Participants must be prepared to assume at least part of the playwright function because the developing dramatic action will be handled most effectively from *within* the event. Experienced practitioners of improvisation are very skilled at managing the action in process, particularly those who work in tightly knit ensembles using prearranged scenarios. Where there is no leader to take a large share in managing the process, the task will be easier when the number of participants is limited. Because controlling and shaping the dramatic invention of three or more participants during the action presents a considerable challenge, the effectiveness of the dramatic action is likely to be in a strict ratio to the number of actors involved. It is apparent that the prevalent mode of interaction in the drama is the dialogue, and this pattern is particularly noticeable in improvisation.

In the work of many improvisation ensembles, the typical method is that two people will begin to develop the pre-text spontaneously, although additional performers may join in. It is not surprising that the control of dramatic action in a large group is problematic even for talented improvisers when even accomplished playwrights choose to structure their work as a series of duets. Working in improvisation with two actors, the British director William Gaskill found it effective to make one responsible for the content and development of the scene; in other words, one actor takes on the playwright function, while the other actor accepts the ideas and assists in developing them.[7] Much of Keith Johnstone's work consists of encouraging actors to accept and build on their partners' ideas rather than "blocking" them or introducing extraneous ideas of their own.

Where there is a large group of participants, as in process drama, the most efficient and aesthetic way to ensure that the crucial playwright function is contained effectively within the ongoing process is for the leader to take on a role in the encounter. When the leader assumes some of the playwright function in this way, the burden on the participants becomes lighter and they can react and respond more freely within the framework provided. They will still be contributing significantly to the growth of the work but are not entirely responsible for its development.

Prearrangement

In every play, it is the predetermined plot that allows the spectator a vantage point from which to observe both the limitations and consequences of the action. Prearrangement and preknowledge of the play's outcome have been seen by some critics as artistically indispensable in the theatre, because this knowledge allows the actors to give the dramatic exchange a satisfying shape. In conventional theatre, actors are faced with the paradox of knowing the conclusion of the play and yet having to act as if anything is possible. The ability to achieve this effect forms a significant part of their technique.

The eventual outcome, in terms of the plot, of many theatre events will be known in advance to the performers and sometimes, particularly in the case of a classic script, to the audience. But the effect of a successful theatre event can never be reduced to the impact of its plot. Ideally a script is made anew in every successive production and even, in a sense, at every performance. Invention, interpretation, discovery, surprise, and error will all be responsible for varying outcomes at every performance. This quality of unpredictability is central to all theatre and particularly to improvisation and, by extension, process drama. For the participants in improvised drama to know the end toward which they are working, as well as every step along the way, would be in direct contradiction to the nature of the activity and its most characteristic and intriguing aspect. In genuinely improvised drama the dramatic exchange is spontaneous. The event is discovered in action rather than planned in advance. The emphasis is always on exploration, on discovering ends, rather than on reaching predetermined destinations.

A prearrangement of the action that is too precisely detailed will always be as contrary to the spontaneous spirit of improvised drama as it is to that of its close relative, play, which many commentators have identified as the first principle of performance. It is obvious that there would be no point in engaging in a game or any other playful activity if the outcome was already precisely determined. Planned outcomes, where there is no possibility of error or surprise, are incompatible with the essential nature of play, process drama, and even theatre. A balance has to be struck in any theatre event between complete unpredictability and absolute control of the material. Process drama is always unpredictable in its development, but an effective pre-text will support and to some degree moderate this unpredictability.

Repeatability

If an improvised experience has been of any significance, the participants and spectators will retain an impression of the occasion after the event, and this impression, or outline, can be seen as a dramatic "product." To the audience, an effective improvised performance will *seem* written even when there is no prior text, as it will to the participants in process drama. When the event has moved, disturbed, or amused the spectators or participants, its effect on them will be very similar to that of a conventional theatre production.

According to some critics, if a theatre event is to have aesthetic validity, an essential requirement is *repeatability*. If the event is not capable of being repeated in some recognizable form, it may not be possible to identify it as theatre. But to demand repeatability in any kind of improvised drama, where the unique quality of the event is an essential factor, is at first sight more problematic. According to Bruce Wilshire,

> We are clearly in the domain of theatre art—and not merely of something theatrically viewed—only when the play is replicable. *Text* should merely mean what is replicable in the work of art, and it should not prejudice us against cases in which nothing is written in advance, or in which something is written as a transcript of what evolved through improvisations in rehearsal or performance.[8]

It is reassuring that Wilshire, unlike Allardyce Nicoll, does not insist on a conventional script. I believe that the requirement that the event should be replicable in some recognizable form is fulfilled by process drama. It is possible for the leader or teacher, using the same starting point or pre-text, to recreate similar relationships, explore similar themes, and reflect on similar issues on a number of different occasions. Although it may share its origins with other experiences, each separate experience will be unique, just as a play script will give rise to any number of distinct productions. *The Haunted House* demonstrates the many possibilities for development within the same dramatic pre-text.

The concept of an enduring text in theatre means something much more fluid and insubstantial than a conventionally written document, a performance text, or even the transcript of an improvised event.

> The only conditions of (the event's) repeatability are that it be remembered by at least one of the participants and that it be enactable by someone. It would seem to generate a "text" even if the "text" is no more than the memories of participants, actors or audience.[9]

Here, the notion of text is no longer that of a script, a prior document that will determine the details of the theatre event. A text in this sense does not necessarily anticipate, control, or generate the dramatic action but is engendered by this action in the minds of the spectators and participants. It leaves behind an after-image, a trace, an outline, that can be recalled and, if necessary, reconstituted in some degree. This "kernel engraved on the memory," as Brook calls it, is surely identical to the recollections of spectators and actors after any significant experience in theatre.[10]

Any significant dramatic event, whether scripted or improvised, will endure in the memory of those involved in the experience, and so will the encounter of process drama. The concept of text as memory may indicate ways in which actors in primitive and popular theatre passed on their improvised scenarios. It will certainly be useful to the leader using process drama, where it is possible for the same pre-text to be recalled and exploited with different groups on separate occasions. On each occasion, the text that is generated may have some similarities, but will also be the particular outcome of a series of unique encounters among the participants.

Texts from Improvisation

Some of the most exciting improvisation in performance was developed in the 1960s and 1970s by Theatre Machine, an improvisation ensemble set up by Keith Johnstone. The kind of explorations in improvisation undertaken by his actors were designed not merely to increase their skill and resourcefulness or to develop interesting scenarios, although these are outcomes of the work, but also to discover the inner structure of theatre and improvisation by engaging in a prolonged experimental encounter with the medium. Johnstone's notions of acceptance, status, and reversal are all essentially *structural* and are all contained within the spontaneous moment of improvisation which is valued for its own sake.[11] The skill and artistry of Johnstone's actors depended, I believe, not just on their creativity but also on the grasp of dramatic structure that they brought to the challenge of improvisation. These qualities were not lost in performance.

When improvisation is designed for performance to an external audience, some kind of routine, score, or partially controlling script may be inevitable in order to ensure an effective and entertaining event. Many successful partially improvised performances are built on performance texts, routines, or *lazzi,* and these provide a measure of continuity. Loose structures, and even comic routines, will support the actors' invention. At Second City, "true" improvisations developed in the more experimental part of the evening may be repeated, shaped, and presented as part of the main show.

Even for skilled and experienced performers, an entire performance based on improvisation will present considerable difficulties. As improvised performances evolve in length and complexity and more actors are included, the need for a script, or at least a basic controlling plan, becomes increasingly urgent. This need, and the pressure to bring their work before the public, led many experimental ensembles to turn their studio research into performance. Improvisation became a means of constructing performances in rehearsal rather than a way of creating the performance spontaneously. Although the kind of theatre event that is constructed from improvised explorations fulfills Wilshire's criteria of repeatibility and prearrangement and generates a text that is possible in some degree to recall and repeat, difficulties of transmission and exact repetition will persist.

Some avant-garde ensembles, notably those led by Richard Foreman and Robert Wilson, tried to compensate for the absence of a controlling plan, script, or strong plot line by relying on ritualistic or ceremonial elements to sustain their performances. They attempted to control the spontaneity of improvisation through the predictability of ritual. These avant-garde directors overlooked fundamental differences between the novelty and immediacy that is typical of improvisation and the essentially "fixed" and highly structured nature of ritual. Inevitably, a powerful effect of the inclusion of ritual elements in theatre is to arouse and control audience involvement in the event, because one of the most significant effects of ritual actions is that they are capable of generating appropriate behavior from others. Ritual is a specific form of action and its function is to stimulate involvement in the occasion among the spectators. But if participation in this kind of activity is to be meaningful, it requires an established ritual familiar to all. It may be impossible for an audience to acquire such familiarity instantly, so the action into which they are drawn is unlikely to have real significance for them.

Ensemble Texts

The theatrical text that evolves from improvised activities frequently belongs quite specifically to the director and the ensemble by whom it has been generated, because the material of the explorations on which it is based arises from the imaginations and psyches of individual actors. There is likely to be an emphasis on powerful visual and ritual elements, and the performance text is inseparable from the living presence of the performers and the environments in which they appear.

Schechner defines the text arising from this kind of work as a score, a total *mise-en-scene:*

> The emphasis in making a performance text is on systems of rela-
> tionships: confrontations, or otherwise, among words, gestures,
> performers, space, spectators, music, light—whatever happens on
> stage.[12]

A celebrated example of a text of this kind is Grotowski's *Apocalipsis cum Figuris.* This performance text evolved out of acting exercises and improvisations designed to facilitate the actors' self-exploration, and continued to develop through a number of distinct versions. The audience, eventually limited to twenty-five in number, was expected to go through the same psychological processes experienced by the actors, but the passivity imposed on the spectators highlighted the fact that this ritual vision of theatre could only be fully effective for the closed community of actors themselves.

Although such events may reverberate powerfully in the memories of those who attended or took part in them, it is doubtful whether any other company or group of actors could repeat or recreate this work in any real sense. Grotowski's subsequent work led to the breakdown of any distinction between actor and audience and the rejection of any separation between the creative process and the creative result. His concerns moved toward what became known as paratheatrical experiments, and, more recently, toward an exploration of the ritual and communal sources of theatrical experiences. It is worth noting that although performance as psychophysiological process may open itself to a broader constituency, the result of this may be that performance as *theatre* is left behind. Grotowski's explorations have become so fundamentally transitional as to lead the company, eventually, out of theatre itself.

Examples of "partly solidified" texts can be found in the work of the Wooster Group, the New York–based ensemble that has collaborated on the development and production of theatre pieces for the past fifteen years. The members claim that the works they present are

> subversive assimilations of old conventions of theatrical realism
> with non-representational and anti-illusionist stage techniques and
> a new naturalism based on ideas and techniques of television and
> film language.[13]

In the process of developing these performances, sources such as Miller's *The Crucible* and Chekhov's *Three Sisters* or writings on the use of LSD are juxtaposed with powerful visual images, fragments of popular culture and social history, as well as events that emerge from the actors' explorations of personal experience. In rehearsal, through a process of editing, cutting, and splicing, the structure of a piece gradually emerges and the various ingredients are fused into a cohesive theatrical form. An element of improvisation and a quality of random selection persist, because new material is added at every performance. As with other avant-garde ensembles, it is extremely unlikely that the work of the Wooster Group could be replicated by other performers or directors.

From Improvised Text to Script

A number of works by such avant-garde theatre artists as Barba, Wilson, Foreman, and Lee Breuer have been published, but this does not necessarily suggest either cohesion or a literary quality to the reader. These printed texts convey very little clear idea of what the theatre events associated with them might have been or what they might become in other circumstances. How far any other group of theatre workers could stage a production of these texts is questionable. They remain outlines, incomplete documents of theatre experiences that would be almost impossible for other groups to reconstitute.

It is certainly possible for a theatrical text that is generated from improvised activities in rehearsal to become as fixed as any other play script, and as capable of being realized theatrically by other actors and directors. It is also important to remember that a theatre event that has evolved from improvisation does not necessarily have to be aligned with the avant-garde. The work of the British director Mike Leigh is a case in point. His plays, which have been televised, published, and staged successfully in the commercial theatre, can be judged in the same way as those of a conventional playwright. Improvisation is the starting point for his actors, who individually develop the fictional lives of their characters. Leigh then turns their explorations into a script by constructing the contexts and situations in which these characters interact. There is no improvisation or spontaneous invention of dialogue during the performance. Leigh claims authorship of each piece, pointing out that although the actors have a great deal of input, "you don't form a committee to decide what the play's going to be about." [14]

Leigh's work, despite the manner of its devising, remains intensely conventional. It is not experimental in any self-conscious sense. His innovations are not primarily to do with the nature or form of the theatre, but with the ways in which the fictional biographies that form the content of his plays are developed. The basically traditional characterizations of his actors could hardly be more different from, for example, the work of performers in Grotowski's ensemble, who develop their roles from improvisations that search for the individual's basic impulses in reaction to the demands of the group situation. They create a personal "score" rather than projecting into the kind of fictional "other" that Leigh's actors develop in exhaustive detail.

It may be worth noting here that Happenings, and much performance art, so often associated with both improvisation and the avant-garde, have little real similarity to improvised drama. Actions in a Happening are indeterminate and inconsequential rather than improvised. Happenings are perhaps more closely related to visual art or dance than to theatre. Not only do all examples have some kind of script or score, but very few use chance procedures, either in composition or performance, and even fewer depend on improvisation or encourage an audience to participate. It is difficult to define Happenings as drama because they typically lack the essential element of human action, whether intended or achieved, and rarely give rise to possible worlds. Where acting is required, it is likely to be of a rudimentary nature. Indeed, even the innovative status of Happenings may be in question. They have been identified as an old form of game, a kind of reinvention of the "Marvels" of the middle ages, whose chief characteristics are that

> its appearance is unexpected, its form unceremonious, and that it erupts into some formal occasion with a pleasurable shock, not unmixed with the horrific.[15]

The revival of this game has been viewed as further confirmation of the decline in the importance of the playwright in modern theatre.

Texts from Process Drama

Process drama, whose nature is primarily defined by the absence of any prior literary document and which finds its meaning and being only in action, will generate a text made up of a similar network of relationships to those forged in any other theatre event. The text generated in process drama will evoke a possible world or at least possess the potential to be translated into a possible world. Significant aspects of this text will be capable of repetition and may even permit a degree of prearrangement. In theory it might be possible to record or transcribe the latent text of process drama, and like any conventional play script, this text will have the capacity to endure in the memory and to generate further improvised events.

New Worlds from Old: Discovering Pre-texts

■ **Effective pre-texts** will launch drama worlds with economy and clarity, but it may not always be easy for the leader or director to identify the most fruitful pre-texts for process drama. The best counsel is to consider the kinds of pre-texts that have generated powerful dramatic action throughout the history of the theatre. Myth, legend, folktale, and historical and topical occurrences provide indispensable pre-texts for dramatists. Sophocles' myths, Shakespeare's history plays, the reworking of biblical stories in Tirso de Molina's *Rape of Tamar* and Peter Shaffer's *Yonadab,* Giradoux's *Amphitrion,* Yeats' *Pot of Broth,* Shaffer's *Equus,* Webster's *Duchess of Malfi,* and countless other greater and lesser plays have exploited and transformed their sources. In their turn, classic plays become pre-texts for other dramatists, as *Antigone* did for Sartre, *Hamlet* for Stoppard's *Rosencrantz and Guildenstern Are Dead,* and *Romeo and Juliet* for Bernstein's *West Side Story.*

The greatest dramatic poets frequently choose to rework existing material. Creative and inventive playwrights do not prize personal invention, but often choose instead to transmit their meanings through preexisting patterns. These ancient motifs and relationships are played out again and again through the ages and still speak freshly to us. They can be revisited in process drama where they support the explorations of the participants as they create and encounter archetypal roles and relationships, as in the following example.

The Crucible

In this session with adults, Gavin Bolton set up a dramatic world that reflects the patterns of power in the pre-text from which he chose to work, Arthur Miller's play *The Crucible.* Bolton's purpose was to show how it is possible to explore significant themes in a classic play by establishing a parallel dramatic world, but an overriding aim was to provide the participants with a significant dramatic encounter.

Episodes	Drama Elements
In an introductory phase of the drama, Bolton mimes the molding of an imaginary wax doll and sticks pins in it, foreshadowing the atmosphere of accusation and superstition that will develop.	This activity has a **ritual** quality. It allows the rest of the participants to remain as **audience** and develop expectations while they experience a representation of the occult at work.
Outside the drama, he asks the group to list their own superstitions, however trivial. Bolton tells the group that the drama will be set in seventeenth-century Salem. The setting of the dramatic world is announced and initiated.	The task is **outside** the imagined world, but builds involvement by relating the theme to the participants' own experience, focuses their anticipation, and provides direct exposition.
Working in family groups, participants create a tableau of the way they would like their children to appear to the community. This task highlights the themes of respectability and community approval that are significant in the original, as well as the deception of appearances.	A **composed**, rather than improvised activity. Each family shares its tableau with the rest of the group as audience. The task sets up an ambiguous image and a **tension** between appearance and reality.
The validity of these representations of respectability are challenged when these family members are interrogated by Bolton in role as the minister in the community. A second phase in this episode heightens the tension and the contrast between appearance and reality when the minister announces that some children have been seen dancing naked in the woods.	This improvised encounter is built on the images presented in the previous episode. The tension in the episode is driven by a **past event** and the **anticipation of future consequences.** There is a growing sense that spying and informing on each other is a regular occurrence in the community. The majority of the participants are spectators during this phase.
Outside the drama, the participants in role as children are asked to	The decision, which is taken individually outside the dramatic

come to a decision about their own guilt or innocence of this charge and write it secretly on a piece of paper. This commits them to a particular point of view.

world, has some of the quality of a **game**, and heightens the **role within a role** that some of the innocent children are playing.

Everyone is called to a church meeting. Bolton, still in role as minister, accuses the children of evil practices and asks them to affirm their innocence publicly in the face of the congregation.

A powerful and theatrical improvised episode, that includes strong **ritual** elements. There is sense of **public spectatorship** as participants "read" the performances of the children.

In family groups, the parents try to discover the truth from their children. The tension in this scene is more personal, and the questioning more intense.

The implications of the previous scene are played out more privately, as **appearance** and **reality** once more conflict.

There is a final confrontation in the church. The minister tries without success to make the guilty ones confess.

In this improvised **tribunal** there is once again a **ritual** quality and a sense of judgement at work.

Outside the drama the children reveal the truth. In some cases, those most suspected by the others turned out to be blameless, and the guilty were most sincere in their protestations of innocence.

These revelations came outside the dramatic world and provoked **reflection** on the events created in this world, as well as on the original play.

The pre-text chosen by Bolton provided powerful parameters for the dramatic world that emerged. The setting, atmosphere, and power relationships of the original text remained intact, as did the atmosphere of spying, accusation, and hysteria that is characteristic of *The Crucible*. The central dramatic encounter was an informal tribunal, a legal process, echoing the trial scene in the play, and questions of control and punishment, guilt and innocence, appearance and reality, and role playing within the role all were key elements in this process drama. The work was valuable in its own right but also provided a powerful approach to the original play.

Transforming the Pre-text

Experimental theatre artists, including Grotowski, Marowitz, Heiner Muller, Schechner, Wilson, and the Wooster Group, freely use classic plays as pre-texts. Dramatic masterworks may be a vital component in their theatre events, but they are not sacrosanct for these innovative directors and ensembles. The texts are not treasured as guardians of a specific meaning to be found, interpreted, and transmitted. Instead, in the light of postmodernism, these plays are "matter awaiting meaning." They are points of departure, "phoenix texts," that become material in a new art work and are played with and explored like objects in a game. As Pavis puts it,

> [P]ostmodern theatre recuperates by reworking the classical heritage and needs classical norms to establish its own identity.[1]

The classic source or pre-text operates as an essential preliminary frame for these artists. The extent and character of the material adopted from the original work may be drastically altered by the inner logic of the rehearsal process. Often the original script may become more or less unrecognizable, although a similar pattern of relationships, tensions, and encounters will persist. Arthur Miller's lawyers took exception to the use of sections of *The Crucible* in a production by the Wooster Group. As a result, changes were made to these "borrowed" portions of the play, but in performance it appeared as if the effect of these minor alterations only served to draw the attention of the audience even more strongly to their origins. One can only speculate about the impact of these borrowings on spectators unaware of the original. Stoppard's *Rosencrantz and Guildenstern Are Dead* involves the audience in an ironic conspiracy of knowledge about both characters and outcomes. An audience unfamiliar with its pre-text, *Hamlet,* however, will be shut out of this conspiracy. The play is likely to give spectators the impression that a much greater drama is taking place backstage.

The particular value of literary classics for Grotowski and his experimental theatre ensemble is in the fact that they already exist as archetypes in the public mind and carry a generalizing resonance that is very close to myth.

> All the great texts represent a sort of deep gulf for us . . . The strength of great works really consists in their catalytic effect: they open doors for us, set in motion the machinery of our self-

> awareness . . . For both producer and actor, the author's text is a
> sort of scalpel enabling us to open ourselves, to transcend our-
> selves, to find what is hidden within us.[2]

A problem arose for Grotowski when his focus on the actor's self-exploration, revelation, and transcendence conflicted with the kinds of
characterization demanded by these plays.

> In *Dr Faustus* the characters were treated as a trampoline, an in-
> strument to study what is behind our everyday mask—the inner-
> most core of our personality—in order to sacrifice it, expose it,
> and the result was to create a deliberate confrontation with the ac-
> tors' own experience.[3]

Here, the script has been used as a kind of springboard challenging
the actor to become an acrobat with the text and to respond to the
writer's creation with his own creative act. The text is used to illuminate the actor's own psyche rather than the other way around. The
original play has not been entirely abandoned, but improvisations and
explorations go beyond mere exercises and have been used to transform the work. Grotowski's word to describe these experiments—*confrontation*—is a useful one, conveying the idea of the dynamic and
almost adversarial relationship of the actors to the text. In Marowitz's
work on *Measure for Measure* described earlier, the courtroom improvisation was also transformative in its extension and elaboration of the
text. Its primary purpose, however, was to allow the actors' insights to
illuminate the characters they were preparing to play.

The purpose of experimental improvised encounters with a previously existing script, in either process drama, rehearsal, or performance, may focus on extending and elaborating the imagined world
of the play. In these cases, parallels, elaborations, and variations of
the characters, settings, and themes of the original script may develop, but the source of these explorations—the original text—will
still resonate strongly within the work. Where the pre-text is a classic
play, it provides atmosphere, genre, situations, tensions, tasks, and
dilemmas that will constrain, focus, and enrich the actors' explorations. In other instances, including those previously described, such
encounters will materially enlarge, distort, or reframe the original
text and the actors' relationship to it. The possibilities of a powerful
pre-text are unlikely to be exhausted by a few brief improvisations. It
will continue to retain a certain power to generate significant dramatic encounters.

Pre-texts operate in many other kinds of improvised drama, both those primarily designed for entertainment and those that are seen as part of the avant-garde. In the earlier example from Second City, a suggestion from the audience functioned as a pre-text, however scant. The words *Hooker* and *Farmer* immediately suggest possible locations and encounters, define roles, and imply relationships. The spectators develop certain expectations about the piece they are to see. The tension of a game underlies the challenge to the performers in the title that has been proposed. It is worth noting that audience suggestions to improvisational ensembles are often potentially and deliberately coarse, obscene, or absurd. A great deal of the delight of the game for the spectators comes in watching the actors struggling to rise above the clichéd nature of the ideas they have been offered and managing to engage genuinely and inventively with these ideas without creating embarrassment for themselves and offending the audience.

Pre–pre-texts

Some of the research or preparation undertaken by actors occurs in advance of the pre-text and becomes a *pre–pre-text*. Examples of this kind of work are the researches of Barba's actors and the explorations of actors working with the British director and playwright Mike Leigh, mentioned earlier. This preparatory material is generally too wide-ranging and unfocused to operate immediately as a useful pre-text. It will require selection and distortion to be transformed into a functional pre-text. In many ensembles this playwright function will be undertaken by the director.

The significance of a pre-text lies in what it *implies* and, above all, in its implication for action. To focus primarily on developing and elaborating a character will not give rise to a pre-text unless the character carries an immediate implication for action. This is most likely to happen in the case of a narrow functional character, one that is easily labeled and whose probable actions are both readily known and obviously circumscribed. To operate as pre-texts, characters must suggest intentions. Functional characters of this kind are obvious dramatic stereotypes. Once again, *The Farmer and the Hooker* from Second City are examples of functional characters of this type. The intentions and actions of the two characters in regard to each other can be assumed to be obvious and are easily (and eagerly) anticipated by the audience.

Transformation and Adaptation

It is not possible merely to accept and use the pre-text as it stands. The leader must choose and build on the pre-text in a particular way. It must be transformed. A frequent misunderstanding, particularly among teachers, is to believe that dramatic experiences will arise by the simple expedient of adapting and dramatizing stories that appear to be appropriate pre-texts. This approach is likely to lead to work that is explanatory rather than exploratory. The pre-text must be sufficiently distorted or reworked so as to be in effect made new, confronted, or transformed.

In the United States, "creative dramatics" was developed by the innovative educator Winifred Ward during the 1920s and 1930s. This approach is strongly based on narrative structure. A simple storyline, often taken from a traditional tale, underpins the activity and provides a straightforward scenario around which the dialogue is improvised by the students with the help of the teacher. But far from encouraging a spontaneous response to the original material or text, what is often required of the children in this approach is actually the reverse of the immediacy and spontaneity of their own dramatic play. Exploration and discovery are necessarily limited, because to work from a storyline implies that there is an "it," the story, which must be replicated. This determines the development of the work. The task is to reproduce the original details of this story as accurately and effectively as possible.

This creative dramatics approach will not necessarily promote any kind of integrated or transformative response to the original material or any wider exploration of the themes of the story. It bears little resemblance to the ways in which innovative theatre workers have used text as a source for generating dramatic meanings. The objectives of the work are adaptation and dramatization rather than transformation. The original story becomes a text to be analyzed and organized, cast, rehearsed, and presented. Worthwhile cognitive, social, and theatrical outcomes may be achieved by the students, but it is important to recognize that this essentially analytical approach is precisely the opposite of the integrative and transformative way in which children engage in make-believe and can be seen almost as a subversion of this impulse. The outcome is an end-product, in effect a piece of informal theatre whose main purpose is to provide a shaped and coherent experience for the watchers, even though these watchers may only be the other members of the class and the teacher. Teachers who attempt to recreate a narrative experience with their students are not transforming the narrative into drama, but into a "representational schema" of what has already taken place.[4]

There are interesting parallels between engagement in drama activities and reader response theory. Louise Rosenblatt identifies two key approaches to engaging with a text. One she defines as "efferent," where the focus is on the information to be gleaned. This is a highly cognitive reading. The other reading is "aesthetic," where the text is encountered for its own sake and the insight and satisfaction that come from engaging with it.[5] In these terms, creative dramatics seems to demand a more efferent reading, while process drama is an aesthetic encounter.

Even where transformation of the original is the aim of the work, not all stories will operate effectively as dramatic pre-texts. Although the themes and characters in a story may seem dramatic, an obstacle exists in the nature of narrative structure which obeys very different laws from those of drama. Reproducing the external features of a story will not necessarily elicit the internal coherence that is characteristic of process drama. As Heathcote emphasizes, stories suggest diachronic time unfolding from past to present, while drama demands synchronic time, a dramatic present, which she defines as the web of interaction within the frame of a selected environment and event.[6] Langer's definition of narrative as the mode of Memory supports this distinction. Unlike narrative structure, which carries a story from its origins up to the present, drama focuses on future consequences and is the mode of Destiny.[7]

Story Drama

It is worth noting here a more genuinely exploratory use of stories as pre-texts for drama that emerged in the 1980s. David Booth, whose work with children's picture books has had a considerable influence on Canadian drama teachers, is a leading exponent of story drama. In this approach, the story or picture book is used as a source of understanding, not as a subject for adaptation or elaboration. It becomes a springboard for meanings developed by the participants, a text to be confronted and transformed.

> Story drama occurs when the teacher uses the issues, themes, characters, mood, conflict or spirit of the story as a beginning for dramatic exploration . . . the action in the story drama develops as the participants solve or work through the dilemma symbolized in the story.[8]

The participants experiment with roles, meet challenges, and solve problems within the imagined world of the story and with the immediacy and spontaneity of improvisation in synchronic time. The following account of a session taught by Booth gives a flavor of the work:

> In the story (*The Dancing Tigers,* by Russell Hoban) the Rajah disturbs jungle life by bringing taped music along on a tiger safari, and in revenge, the tigers dance the Rajah to death. How this occurs is unclear in the book . . .
>
> I went into role as the Rajah's son who had returned from America to discover the reason for his father's death. The children in role as the trackers and servants gave me various explanations about his death, conjectured from their own knowledge and unrelated to the story. Eventually, two students volunteered the information that the Rajah had been danced to death. I, in role, angrily rejected their responses, claiming that I no longer accepted such superstitious beliefs since I had been educated in America. It was now up to the students to prove the truth of the story to me, since I had ordered them all locked up until they disclosed the real reason for his death.
>
> The son then left the room, and I, as teacher, worked with the students in groups as they set about planning to help the son to understand what had happened on that safari.
>
> When we returned to role, the children demanded the opportunity to prove that the father had indeed died from the dancing tigers. They asked the son to accompany them on a similar safari. . . Then two boys, as tigers, began the Dance of the Silence that is Partner to the Violence. As we watched, I was suddenly taken by both arms and asked politely to leave the tigers or I would meet my father's fate.[9]

In this example, there is no attempt to reenact the narrative. Instead, the teacher takes on a role, the experience is a genuine dramatic encounter, and the students' decisions and responses determine the development of the event. The children's challenge to the teacher in role parallels that in the original story without merely imitating it. They may not be able to explain their understanding of this mysterious event discursively, but they have responded imaginatively and dramatically and have entered and interacted with the imagined world of the story. They have generated a new text and had a unique dramatic experience.

In story drama, the original story operates as a genuine pre-text and provides a starting point for these explorations. Its existence gives confidence to the teacher and supports and validates the efforts of the participants. The story provides, in effect, a structuring framework without becoming a narrative straightjacket, and the activities include both elaboration and transformation. In such transformative explorations, the original text has not been entirely abandoned, but the relationship of the participants to the original is materially altered. In story drama, the participants are given the opportunity of interrogating, confronting, and transforming the text. The original story becomes a powerful pretext for their explorations.

Pre-text, Stimulus, and Focus

The significance of the pre-text in generating effective explorations has been recognized in many handbooks on improvisation and, particularly, drama in education, some of which consist of very little else. These handbooks may suggest potential courses of development for the action beyond the pre-text. Others will emphasize the pre–pretext by providing materials for research, original documents, pictures, and extracts from scripts. The publication of material of this kind clearly indicates that the resulting improvisation can be recalled and repeated, even if the growth of the resulting dramatic world is likely to take a different shape on each occasion. All of this material can be useful to the teacher or director, but it is essential to understand the way in which pre-texts should be employed if the dramatic world is to develop satisfactorily. The essential skill of the director or experienced improviser in theatre, or of the drama teacher and her students in the classroom, is to take a pre-text and rapidly discover the dramatic action that it implies.

It is important to be able to recognize the difference between material that will operate as a pretext and that which remains merely a stimulus. Without the inherent functional and structural features of a pre-text, as I defined them earlier, the drama will not easily be initiated, maintained, or developed. A term closely related to this notion of pre-text is *focus*. This term has been popular in the past with drama teachers, but is usually defined too loosely and variably to prove really serviceable. It is often used both as verb and noun, almost in the same breath. The attempt to initiate improvised drama has been described as "finding the focus," as if this focus, once found, will satisfactorily drive and structure the activity. It has sometimes been employed to include the educational aims of the drama teacher as well as indicating the theme or direction of the lesson.[10] As Dorothy Heathcote uses it, the term *focus* indicates a principle of selection, definition, distortion, and elaboration, and this is likely initially to be the responsibility of the teacher or leader. What is implied in the way she and Gavin Bolton use the term is the capacity to translate an idea or theme into dramatic action. As Bolton points out, it is the responsibility of the teacher or leader, operating as a playwright, to find a focus that creates an imperative tension and provides a vehicle for the themes and images to be explored. If the pre-text is appropriate and dramatic, the problem of finding the focus will disappear. Dramatic tension will already be implied, roles suggested, and action anticipated.

The Dramatic Heritage

It is possible to confront and transform the great themes of our dramatic heritage through the choice of particular pre-texts. In genuinely transformative approaches, the original text may be recast and reworked and become more or less unrecognizable, although trace elements will persist in the new work in its themes, images, and patterns of relationships. Valuable pre-texts for process drama occur in folktales, fairytales, myths, and historical incidents, as well as in classic literary texts and B-movies, all of which lend themselves to exploration, confrontation, and transformation. The most successful pre-texts for process drama will resonate with the elements and archetypes that have been the life blood of theatre, and indeed popular culture, through the ages. Myth and archetype never merely reside in remote and seemingly irrelevant tales of long ago. Their powerful echoes still wait to wake us through the pre-texts we employ. These archetypal and essentially dramatic threads in the work will connect it with a wider theatre heritage and the literary, mythic, and dramatic legacy of other cultures as well as with soap operas and popular movies, where archetypes clearly persist. Both our craft and our imagination is nourished—whether we acknowledge it or not—by our dramatic ancestors. If we strip ourselves of these connections, this broader frame of reference, we will disinherit ourselves and our students. It is foolish to limit ourselves to the kind of themes that are dramatic in the journalistic, topical, or sensational sense, or educational in a limiting and instrumental way. If we do, we risk restricting our explorations to the commonplace, superficial, or heavily didactic.

When we select pre-texts that resonate with our dramatic and cultural heritage, not with a view to accumulating facts or repeating understandings but with a sense of recognition, of interrogation, we are discovering occasions for understanding, integration, interpretation, and inquiry. Appropriate pre-texts will allow us to encounter and transform the materials of other cultures without necessarily appropriating them. When we create significant dramatic contexts we are building the kind of dramatic curriculum that invites creation, participation, and appreciation. These contexts will give rise to both exploration and performance, promote response and judgement, and resonate with a wide range of other theatre forms.

I found that *The Trojan Women* became a powerful pre-text for process drama with students studying the text in college. The students took on the roles of innocent civilians left behind after the fall of Troy. In role as a representative of the conquerors, the teacher offered them a choice between freedom and slavery. They could choose freedom, but they would have to leave their children with the conquerors. The work became very intense, as grandparents, parents, and older siblings tried to explain their dilemma to the children. After the decision had been made, they were all asked to imagine that they had the power of Cassandra—to be able to foretell the future, but not be believed. Each of them devised their own vision of their future in the light of the decision they'd come to, some in prose, some almost as a ritual incantation. One African-American student made the decision to kill herself and her child rather than allow it to fall into slavery. This choice finds echoes in literary heritage from the Bible and Greek drama to Toni Morrison's *Beloved,* and the plight of innocent victims of war is echoed every day in the news.

In this work, the students were becoming not merely consumers but *producers* of text. The context was certainly part of theatre and literary heritage, but equally it was both historical and topical. The group was also building the syntax of the text—an understanding and exploration of the situation in which the original Trojan women found themselves, a grasp of the genre of the original text and the beginnings of a dramatic style. Where appropriate, these insights may be confirmed in performance.

For those hoping to exploit the full potential of process drama, the identification and transformation of pre-texts that possess true dramatic power and possibility is the first step toward the creation of significant experience.

Scenes and Episodes: Defining the Drama World

■ **Every work of art** gives access to a self-contained imaginative universe, a dramatic "elsewhere." This is most obviously the case in theatre, where the imaginary world is made manifest before our eyes through the human presence of the actors. Imagined worlds, dramatic purposes, aesthetic elements, and formal structures occur in much the same way in process drama as they do in any piece of conventional theatre. These worlds, purposes and structures are created and sustained primarily by the words and actions of the participants and carry within them the potential for further development and articulation. The existence of these dramatic worlds does not depend on the necessity that the participants' words have been determined in advance and will not be invalidated by the fact that their development is spontaneous and unpredictable.

Both theatre and process drama depend on the temporary acceptance of an illusion—a closed, conventional, and imaginary world that exists in the voluntary conspiracy between audience and actors. They both require the participants to engage in active make-believe with regard to objects, actions, and situations; they occur within their own frontiers of time and space; they involve the adoption of roles, demand a degree of interaction, and are firmly set apart from the reality of everyday life. They are temporary worlds existing within the everyday world and are dedicated to the performance of an act apart. Once these worlds and acts have been generated, they persist as creations of the mind, treasures of the memory, and, as established earlier, may be readily recalled and, to some degree, repeated.

In the theatre, the task for the dramatist is to alter at a stroke our customary orientation to both time and space and locate us firmly in an alternative world, the dramatic elsewhere. In process drama the leader is faced with the same task. To achieve it with economy and

immediacy, the best course is to examine the means by which successful dramatists bring the dramatic world into being.

BARNARDO:	Who's there?
FRANCISCO:	Nay, answer me. Stand and unfold yourself.
BARNARDO:	Long live the King!
FRANCISCO:	Barnardo?
BARNARDO:	He.
FRANCISCO:	You come most carefully upon your hour.
BARNARDO:	'Tis now struck twelve. Get thee to bed, Francisco.

This is how Shakespeare sets the world of Hamlet in motion. The elements he deploys are darkness, secrecy, watchfulness, and anticipation. He establishes most economically and dramatically the time, the
place, the mood of suspicion and depression, the tasks and roles of
the characters, and the existence of a King. Shakespeare's pre-text
for *Hamlet* was an old tale many times retold (and perhaps an earlier
play on the same subject by Kyd), and he uses it to draw us into the
world of Elsinore, where the ghost of a murdered king stalks the
battlements. Notice that we find ourselves *in* the world before we
learn any of its details through direct exposition. These details
emerge as we listen, and we have to make sense of them. From the
moment the play begins, we speculate, make assumptions, and develop expectations about the world unfolding before us. In retelling
the events as narrative, this first scene of *Hamlet* would almost certainly be omitted, as would the role of the soldier, Francisco, who
never appears again. All we learn of him is that he is "sick at heart."
But *Hamlet* is not merely the unfolding of a tragic story. It is the experience of a series of increasingly intense dramatic moments and
emotional states, including the first moment on the windswept battlements of Elsinore when we, the spectators, discover the kind of
world into which we are being drawn.

At the beginning of every play, the audience is working almost
harder than the actors, seizing hints, grasping at clues, asking questions, speculating about relationships. The details of the world
emerge gradually on the stage, are subject to change, and are not
fully known until the drama is complete. The dramatic world defines
itself in *action* rather than being set up from outside.

Marlowe launches the imagined world of *Dr. Faustus* in quite a
different way. Here the Chorus narrates the autobiography of
Faustus up to the point where the play begins and then introduces us
to "the man that in his study sits," plunging us immediately into

Faustus' spiritual and intellectual struggle. We hear a highly stylized account of his encounters with the different branches of learning, and the action of the play begins at the point where he makes the decision to embrace forbidden knowledge.

The significance of these early moments, when we as audience are trying to make meaning from the appearances before us, is highlighted in *The Real Inspector Hound,* Tom Stoppard's parody of the country house mystery, a genre not known for its dramatic power and subtlety. Mrs. Drudge, the housekeeper, is dusting, but obviously waiting for the phone to ring.

MRS DRUDGE: Hello, the drawing room of Lady Muldoon's country residence one morning in early spring? Hello! The draw– Who? Who did you wish to speak to? I'm afraid there is no one of that name here, this is all very mysterious and I'm sure it's leading up to something, I hope nothing is amiss for we, that is Lady Muldoon and her houseguests, are here cut off from the world, including Magnus, the wheelchair ridden half-brother of her ladyship's husband Lord Albert Muldoon who ten years ago went out for a walk on the cliffs and was never seen again—and all alone, for they had no children.

The deliberate clumsiness of this exposition of plot and the way in which Stoppard cleverly parodies the clichés and incompetence of less accomplished writers actually draws attention to the skill of playwrights who draw us into the action dramatically and economically.

Story and Plot

Plot is *not* synonymous with story, although from the beginnings of dramatic theory, critics have agreed that every dramatic text is essentially founded on a story. A story has three essential elements—human or anthropomorphic subjects and dimensions of time and space. These elements represent the structure of invariable relationships that always occur in every rendering of a particular story. The simplest account of the plot of any dramatic text already contains important structural elements and networks of relationships. A dramatic plot often includes a powerful element of causality. It will have the three essentials of the story—human subjects, a setting, and a temporal dimension—but it will also include *action*. The subjects make deliberate decisions that have consequences, and choices that bring about a change in the situation.

The essentially simple outlines of structurally satisfying plots are readily available to the leader in process drama. These may include a move from one relationship to its opposite, from a prediction or fear to its opposite, from a problem to its solution, from a misrepresentation to a rectification. The arc that the pre-text has initiated is completed in the circle of the action.

For Aristotle, the plot represented a unified, self-contained causal context. This notion of a closed dramatic structure presenting a causally linked series of opposed actions and counteractions has been overturned in contemporary theatre theory and practice. Instead of a linear, causally linked, single plot sequence, open forms of dramatic structure have been recognized and developed. These forms tend to replace a sense of linear finality with a series of cyclical repetitions and variations. Here, the scene is the decisive structural unit and the work is structured from its constituent parts to the complete text.

Episodic Development

An important element in the structural transformation of any story into a plot is the way in which the dramatic presentation is divided into segments. The first step toward solving the problem of structure in process drama lies in conceiving of the development of the work in units or episodes. Organizing their work into a number of episodes is a familiar procedure for drama teachers, who choose from a variety of dramatic modes and employ a wide range of exciting strategies in order to engage participants in the imagined world of the drama. This notion of episodic development is often neglected in the kind of improvisation used in actor training and rehearsal.

In my own experience, the journey toward an understanding of theatre form began with the realization that dramatic development did not necessarily imply a linear narrative. Once I had grasped the idea that the drama could develop in an episodic or panoramic fashion through a series of significant encounters, it became clear that a number of formal aesthetic and dramatic features were involved in the creation and development of the imagined world.

Although the leader in a drama session may be capable of conceiving of the event in episodes and choosing from among different dramatic modes, these possibilities alone may not lead to significant experience for the participants. The recurring challenge to the leader is to select, *during* the process, the kind of episode or scene that will promote the development of the event to a satisfactory fulfillment. It is important to remember that this selection procedure is not a question of deciding in advance on a sequence of episodes so that there is a kind of fixed scenario within which the participants improvise. If the event is to remain essentially improvisatory—implying spontaneity, uncertainty, ingenuity, exploration, and discovery—the sequence of episodes or scenes will not be predetermined, but *discovered* in response to the developing demands of the work. There is a kind of aesthetic necessity in operation. When in theatre we are led to expect an event, that is dramatic likelihood. When we demand an event, that is dramatic necessity. The necessary is most effective when it is presented in the form of the accidental. The attitude of mind in the spectator is what makes a dramatic event credible, and that attitude is created by the genre of which the work is a part as well as by the train of circumstances leading up to that event. The most effective way of accomplishing this sense of dramatic necessity is for the playwright function to be exercised largely from *within* the experience.

Little Red Riding Hood

In this process drama, the pre-text is a very familiar tale, and one that has been retold and reworked in many versions over the years. It was a secure starting point for adolescents unaccustomed to this way of working. The first phases of the process are exercises, and the dramatic world takes firm hold only when the teacher takes on a role and begins to structure the experience from within.

Narration: The students narrate the story of Little Red Riding Hood together, allowing for differing versions and alternate endings to the tale.

Episodes	Drama Elements
The group divides into pairs, A and B. The teacher, in role as editor of a tabloid newspaper, asks the As to go to the village near the woods and interview a local person in order to establish the real facts of the case. The Bs become the locals, typical gossips with lots of opinions about the events. They enjoy elaborating on the facts.	The teacher's role is a way of giving instructions and establishing a context for the task. Participant roles are limited and clichéd, but safe, and provide a means of developing a new perspective on this familiar story. They may elaborate on the original story, develop opinions, and indulge in speculation.
The editor calls the reporters together and gets feedback on the interviews. A large variety of	The teacher's role here is vestigial, but allows for feedback, discussion, and validation of the previous task.

interpretations are offered, and although they cannot all be true, there is obviously something going on. There is a need for more information, especially photographs.

In small groups of four or five, tableaux are created. These show incidents in the woods or the village and are often either sensational or ambiguous. At this stage there is no need to reconcile opposing views of what might have taken place.

Now, there is a distinct change in the dynamic of the work. The dramatic world begins to grow in improvisation. The group sits in a large circle. The teacher in role introduces herself as Sarah Green, the press secretary at the Research Institute near Hood Woods, run by Professor Robinson. She asks that as responsible journalists, the group should repudiate the ridiculous gossip being spread about wolves in the woods. All this adverse publicity is preventing Professor Robinson from completing his important research. The journalists refuse to comply and ask questions about the professor's work, his background, his source of funding, and the relationship between him and Ms. Green. She parries their questions, because she claims to know very little about his research, except that it does not involve genetic manipulation. His purpose is to explore the limits of intelligence. The journalists are highly suspicious of everything the professor is doing and inquire about security and attacks on local people.

Half the group is **audience** to the other half, as they retell what they have heard.

The groups view each other's tableaux and comment on what they see, both for the information the tableaux contain and for the formal qualities of their composition. Once again, the small groups are **audience** to each other's work, but in a more formal sense.

The structure of this episode is oppositional. The group is being asked to do something, to which it refuses to agree. The group accepts its generic "journalist" role, a development from that of "reporter" in the previous task. Some identify themselves as from particular journals, such as *Nature*. Once again, there is speculation and interpretation of Ms. Green's limited responses. The group adds detail and builds the dramatic world by bringing up negative aspects of the professor's previous history as a challenge to Ms. Greene. The game here is to extract information from the leader, who continues to be evasive. It is this evasive attitude that provokes the group into inventing details and adopting a **playwright** function.

Finally, the journalists demand to speak to the professor, and Ms. Green grudgingly agrees to ask him to allow them access to the Research Institute without promising them that they will meet the professor.

Out of role, the teacher and the group reflect on the previous episode and voice their main concerns about the Research Institute.

This reflection is retrospective, and the teacher avoids encouraging too much speculation and building of detail outside the work.

The teacher narrates the next section. The professor has agreed to allow the journalists to visit the Research Institute. She asks the participants to close their eyes and imagine the outside appearance of the Institute. The consensus is that the place has a sterile, scientific appearance; security is clearly in evidence, and there has been an attempt to conceal the existence of the place. This "imaging" is a kind of mental scene painting, and surprising, coherent images arise.

The class is divided into groups of four. The teacher selects one person from each group and asks them to leave the room. She tells the others that the professor wants them to prepare three questions to ask him.

The teacher carefully chooses these "volunteers" for their ability to sustain a difficult role, physically as well as verbally.

Next, she talks privately to the volunteers. These are to be the professor's research subjects, the wolves. In every respect they are fully grown wolves physically, but they are all supremely intelligent, and tremendously gentle. They are devoted to the professor and are happy to be at the Institute because they know no other life. The journalists are asked to leave the room, while the wolves reenter. They establish themselves separately, lying on the floor to indicate their physical difference, as if they are in their dens. They are not in cages.

These participants have a difficult task. They must physically present themselves as wolves, while allowing the rest of their group to discover that they can speak and are very intelligent. They are cautioned not to do too much of the work in the interaction by "telling their stories," but, if necessary, to respond to difficult questions with questions of their own.

The journalists are told that they will meet the subjects of the professor's research, who are, in fact, wolves. These animals are quite tame, and the journalists are in no danger. They will remain in their groups of three and each group will visit one animal, observe it, and form their own impressions.

This is a difficult and sensitive encounter, which may run for ten or fifteen minutes. There is a strong element of **watching**.

Each group of three goes to a wolf, and begins to observe and interact with it. Some rapidly discover that the animal can speak, others never realize this.

Some groups immediately establish a rapport with their wolf. Others remain at a distance, commenting and observing.

Ms. Green interrupts, as the animals now are required for a training session. She asks the journalists to get together to discuss their first impressions. They are very disturbed about what they have seen, and its implications. They believe that this work is highly unnatural and that the wolves have been brainwashed in some way.

The encounter, although bizarre, has been a genuine encounter, and many of the journalists are deeply disturbed by it.

Out of role, she calls the wolves together and asks the journalists to remain in a circle surrounding the wolves, who are sitting on the floor. The wolves discuss their impressions of the journalists. They find them simple-minded, obsessed with questions of sex, curious, patronizing, and generally disappointing. However, they are grateful to the professor for providing them with this new learning experience.

During this debriefing session, the journalists are an **audience**. The change of activity allows them time to begin to deal with their feelings. But as they listen to the wolves' opinion of them, this is even more uncomfortable for the journalists. It is less than flattering, and they see how they have misinterpreted the wolves' responses.

The journalists discuss what they have heard. They are embarrassed to reflect on their easy stereotyping of the wolves, but are still determined that this work should be made public.

They reflect in role and begin to come to some understanding of the creatures they have encountered.

Each time this process drama has taken place, a different sequence of episodes happens at this point. Some groups are interested in investigating the actual education of the wolves and create scenes of the professor working with his strange students. Others follow the suggestion in the original tale of a relationship between a wolf and a human being and develop episodes that show this relationship blossoming, along with its consequences. Others, as the journalists, invite the wolves into their homes in an effort to explain the human world to them. Others imagine the possibility of the wolves escaping to the wilds and attempting to share their knowledge with their own species. Depending on the direction that the work takes, it may or may not be appropriate to include the next part of the sequence. If it is omitted, the new items and final memorial to the professor may still be appropriate episodes to bring some sense of resolution to the drama.

Another sharp change marks the next phase of the work. Out of role, the teacher informs the group that they are now members of the Cabinet, who have been called to an emergency meeting in Washington.

These roles are the most powerful the group has undertaken so far. They now have the power to make decisions.

The teacher, now in role as a Government aide, reminds them that they will have heard of the work of Professor Robinson. Unfortunately, the professor, his mind unhinged by the recent pressures and accusations from the media, has taken his own life. He has also destroyed all of his research notes. No one else knows how he achieved his results. The group has to decide what to do with the wolves at the Research Institute.

During this episode, the participants select specific roles and responsibilities for themselves. Defense, Agriculture, Education, Environment, and Health are among the offices that they claim, and each has a different perspective on the wolves' fate. The debate is heated, and the teacher in role is little more than a moderator in the discussion.

As a way of resolving the deadlock, the next task is to create in small groups a TV news item, set some time in the future, that will clearly show what fate was decided for the wolves. This need not be stated directly, but it should be possible to deduce from the news item what has happened in the interim.

This episode is **composed** and rehearsed rather than improvised. It allows the participants to avoid having to agree on the wolves' fate, but to show alternate endings to their story—in effect, to write the end of the play. The groups are **audience** to each other's presentations.

As a final, reflective task, the entire group, working together, creates a monument to the professor. It allows an abstract representation of some of the themes of the drama.

This is a version of the **tableau**, but devised without any discussion or rehearsal. Everyone takes up a position with regard to everyone else and the effect of the whole composition.

This process drama used a very familiar story as a pre-text, but took off into a very different dramatic world. The only remnants of the original tale were talking wolves, the setting of the woods, and a vestigial sense of a community hostile to the wolves.

The initial exercises allowed the participants a great deal of latitude in elaborating on the original tale. The leader introduced the idea of the Research Station and, subsequently, the death of the professor. Within these constraints, the participants provided details of an imagined past and the physical setting, negotiated the encounter with the wolves, made decisions about their future, and represented the outcomes of that decision. Both the leader and the group had many freedoms within the framework, but were also required to accept, from within the work, certain limitations on their roles and actions. The experience can be a powerful one, for journalists and wolves alike. The encounter with the wolves is one of real tension and unease. It produces fascination and a degree of empathy, but this is challenged when the journalists come to realize that the wolves are more intelligent than the humans they meet, and hold more "civilized" values. The work raises questions to do with freedom, integration, the relationship of humans toward other species, and the responsibility of science. Participants often reflect on the way the drama provides an aesthetically distanced but forceful analogy for exploring attitudes to physical, cultural, or racial differences.

Scenes

The success of this process drama, as well as of the other examples provided in this book, rests on an effective and familiar pre-text that is transformed and elaborated through a careful selection of episodes or scenes, each of which is designed to take the participants deeper into the world of the drama.

The primary unit of dramatic structure is the scene, and one of the first steps in understanding the form and analyzing the structure of a play is the discovery of its component parts or scenes. Once the work has moved beyond the brief skit or exercise, it is possible to analyze it in terms of the units, scenes, or episodes of which it is composed, and their relationship to the whole event. Because of the immediacy and spontaneity of much of process drama, this will be largely a retrospective activity. But an understanding of the way in which scenes can relate to each other, and of the way in which units of action may be chosen to develop the theme, plot, or characters, will enable the work to develop depth and complexity and move toward significant experience.

Dramatic scenes have been defined by commentators in a number of different ways. In classic French drama, scene division occurred when anything happened to change the group onstage, for example, the exit or entrance of a character. In this approach, the scene is defined by the presence of an unchanging group of players. Here is a less exact but perhaps more useful division that has relevance for the episodes in process drama.

> A scene is any narrative unit that, having its own beginning, middle and end, stands out in the over-all pattern of action as a self-contained sequence of events.[1]

Dramatists work out their purposes in terms of the scenes into which their plays are divided. These scenes are social encounters, not merely among the actors involved, but also between the actors and the audience. The dramatist must draw the audience as soon as possible into a state of intense concern with the event, while at the same time building the dramatic world. The leader or drama teacher working in process drama has exactly the same task to accomplish.

The leader or teacher of the group, probably working for at least part of the time in role within the experience, is likely to be primarily responsible for making structural decisions both before and during the experience. These decisions may include selecting or negotiating the pre-text, taking on a role, framing the drama, endowing the participants with roles, and structuring the development of the work from within. When the teacher works in role, the participants have time to contemplate the unfolding dramatic impulse until they are drawn into the experience. As participants become engaged in the experience and develop an interest in and commitment to the work, they are likely to take an increasingly large part in these structural decisions.

Each episode or scene in process drama must take a number of features into account. Many will be based on an encounter of some kind—the whole group with the leader in role, as in *The Haunted House,* or the townspeople with their minister in *The Crucible.* Encoun-

ters may be public, as in these examples, or private, as when Frank
Miller meets his son. They may also take place in small groups, for
example, when the journalists come face to face with the wolves.

A key element in selecting episodes that will move the action forward is dramatic time. This is a fundamental consideration in structuring the unfolding event and will be explored in greater depth in
Chapter 6. An understanding of the complexities of dramatic time, as
well as a sufficient duration of actual time, makes it possible to solve
problems of participation, maintain distance, allow for reflection, and
yet sustain the essentially spontaneous development of the event.

The first scene of *Frank Miller* contained a powerful tension between the past, in which Frank had been wronged by the townspeople, and the unknown future, in which he might take revenge on
them. The second episode, in tableaux, created Frank's past, not in
terms of plot details but as an elaboration of his character. Then the
action returned to the present, now further filled with the tension of
Frank's hidden presence in the community and his equally obscure
purposes. This backtracking is similar to the way in which the plot of
Oedipus unfolds, where we hear explanations of events that happened twenty years previously. The story backtracks and then moves
forward again. This movement toward the future, in terms of the consequences of previous actions rather than a preoccupation with what
happens next, gives rise to the kind of expectations required to drive
the work forward. Time need not operate in a linear way, but may reveal the event episodically or panoramically. Episodes or scenes will
not merely succeed one another in a straightforward chronological
sequence. Each segment will have an appropriate temporal dynamic
and be oriented toward the past, present, or future. Any process
drama, like any play, includes moments of intense "living through"
experience, reflective or contemplative passages, the manipulation of
time both backward and forward, changes of pace and tempo, and
episodes of greater or lesser tension and intensity.

In order to develop the background to an event or to understand a
character's history, the work may include an orientation toward the
past—two people share a memory, tableaux are created of a significant
incident or an important moment of decision, an incident is recalled or
relived in a dream. For moments of greatest tension, scenes that are
powerfully in the present may be chosen—a confrontation or encounter; a challenge, surprise, or reversal; a trial or a decision. When there
is a need to develop a sense of what is to come, of the form being fulfilled, the action might include preparations for an important occasion,
prophetic foreshadowings in dreams, omens or appearances, or the

enactment of shared hopes for the future. All of these possibilities are familiar to dramatists who struggle to give form to their material and may be used with equal success in process drama.

One of the most difficult decisions to make in the unfolding process is that of selecting the final episode. Because of the exploratory and sometimes fragmentary nature of the work, there may be a need in the final scenic unit to reflect on and sum up what has gone before. The emphasis may be contemplative (as in looking back on the different stages of Frank Miller's development) or celebratory (a memorial to those involved). Some material will lend itself to completion in an epilogue—through a scene or encounter ten years after the events that have been explored, or through an ironic commentary on the action—perhaps in the form of narration. An example of the use of time to provide a satisfying sense of fulfillment occurs in *The Seal Wife*, the process drama that is described in Chapter 5. It was suggested to the participants that so much time had passed that the events only persisted as dim memories in the minds of the people and had been transformed into another medium, a folk dance.

The Rules of the Game

The dramatic world cannot happen without agreement to complicity in the creation of that world. The leader must first of all engage the participants in the event, and then encourage them to contribute to the development of the dramatic world so that it becomes a group creation articulated through the growth of an imaginative consensus. Agreement and cooperation among participants are fundamental before any kind of competitive or interactive encounter can take place. Children's play and competitive games are full of encounters—cops with robbers, doctors with nurses, knights with queens, forwards with backs—and these are essentially social and interactive. These encounters will be neither satisfying nor coherent unless there is an acceptance of the game and its explicit or implicit rules. The encounters of dramatic characters on the stage with each other and with the audience also depend on agreement and acceptance. Competition, opposition, and display all provide aspects of the necessary tension of any game including the "game" of theatre, but agreement to play the game and consensus about the kind of game that is being played are prerequisites for the activity. In conventional theatre, the script provides actors with information about the kind of world they are creating, and they display their understanding and agreement to build this world together by the coherence of the style they adopt. This sense of a coherent style can also develop strongly in process drama, especially where the pre-text emphasizes a dominant mood or atmosphere and the leader in role models appropriate language and bearing for the participants. The urgency and anxiety of the leader in *Frank Miller* is quickly caught and echoed by the group, and part of the game is to try to discover as much as possible about Frank and his relationship to the group without *directly* asking for information. A sense of the genre in which they are working will be particularly important if participants in process drama are to maintain both a style and the direction of the work that arises from the initial consensus. As well as developing the dramatis personae who "people" the imagined world, the participants may become mental scene painters, creating the physical and atmospheric features of this world through their verbal descriptions and physical realizations. In *Frank Miller,* the participants created through their imaging both the appearance of the town and the period in which the event occurred. Specific locations, such as the saloon and the livery stables, were described by the group, and their physical properties were suggested by a simple rearrangement of the available furniture. Even the negotiation of these small details of the imagined world will build consensus so that it becomes increasingly a group creation. The dramatic world of either theatre or process drama cannot come into being unless the spectators and participants acknowledge their essential collusion in the creation of that world.

Working from Within

For improvised dramatic activities to achieve their potential as more than mere training or rehearsal procedures, educational tools, or the occasions for superficial displays of skill—in other words, to become what I have described as process drama—the developing dramatic action must be handled effectively from *within* the event in a manner that respects the rules of the medium. These rules, like those of any other art process, are best assimilated by prolonged exposure to the medium. Francis Fergusson is one of the few commentators to recognize the value of improvised activities in promoting a knowledge of drama and its underlying forms.

> When skilled actors improvise a playlet upon an imagined situation, they respond freely to each other's actions and words within it, yet never violate its basic *données*.[2]

What Fergusson is pointing out is the operation of inner rules within the process. Theatre also works through the application of internal and external rules and conventions. It is these rules and conventions that establish and control the development of the dramatic world in both theatre and process drama. As soon as a make-believe world comes into being, even at the level of children's dramatic play, a number of possibilities are immediately eliminated and the rules and conventions of the genre begin to control its development. There are immediate demands on the participants to act against impulse according to the developing constraints of the make-believe situation, or in other words, according to the rules of the game. Responses are free within the limits of these rules, and satisfaction for the participants comes from the discovery of appropriate responses, which, although subject to acceptance and modification by the contributions of the other players, exploit this latitude. Only responses that promote the growth of the dramatic world will be acceptable. The rules of the games in theatre are already known to the spectators who collude with them, but in improvisation and process drama, as in dramatic play, these rules are discovered or generated in action. As Spolin notes, the purpose of rules is to keep the players playing.[3]

The existence and significance of rules and conventions are revealed most clearly when they are broken. Many dramatists have chosen to shatter the accepted rules of theatre and thereby drawn attention to them—from the grocer and his wife who interrupt the play in *The Knight of the Burning Pestle* to Pirandello's resentful characters in search of an author and the shock tactics of avant-garde theatre groups. Postmodern theatre practices focus on the breaking of these rules and celebrate the shattering of audience expectation by calling into question the key features of theatre that I have been considering, as well as the existence of both subject and meaning.

The deep affiliations between play and theatre are clearly displayed in the fundamental vocabulary of the drama. Like dramatic play, process drama generates a tension between freedom and necessity, spontaneity and structure. Both process drama and theatre are bracketed from real life, although the physical location of most theatre events will make this bracketing less equivocal that the more fluid arrangements of improvised events. All three modes—play, process drama, and theatre—are bounded in time and space and require that the actual situation, the real context, be to some degree masked, concealed, suppressed, constrained, and controlled so that particular aspects of human behavior may be selected, defined, and articulated within the virtual world, without constraints other than those imposed by the laws of the medium. Representation and display are key elements of each of these modes, and even competition, that essential aspect of any game, will to some degree be present.

Managing Dramatic Action

Although an effective pre-text will set a dramatic world in motion, and although the participants may be capable of discovering the rules of the game in action, the leader, director, or teacher is still faced with the problem of managing the dramatic action from within the unfolding process. This is also the essential task of the dramatist. Action is the basic medium of theatre and the channel through which ideas are projected. It will be just as important for the leader and participants in process drama to be able to understand and manipulate the power of the dramatic activity in which they are engaged as it is for the dramatist who sets up dramatic action for others.

As discussed earlier, there is a powerful tendency for drama to be structured through a sequence of duets. Whatever the number of characters on stage, playwrights tend to align them so that they share a common active or reactive thrust. Where an improvisation is structured as a duet, the majority of the participants are relegated to being merely spectators to the exchange. But this encounter can be managed in a different way. The pre-text may be provided by the teacher in role, which is one of the most effective and economical means of activating the dramatic world. The dramatic exchange then takes place between the teacher in role and the other members of the group, who have been bound together in unity and are now being brought into active participation in the event. The exchange, in effect, remains a duet, involving action and reaction.

> Although the number of persons increases, the dramatic impulse emitted by one actor and directed at another does not multiply . . . the interchange of impulses rather than the mere number of bodies should be noted.[4]

The use of teacher in role is one of the most productive and succinct ways of initiating the interchange of impulses that is at the heart of dramatic action. It is also the clearest example of the way the teacher or leader may adopt a playwright function within the improvised process in order to activate a pre-text and begin the weaving of the dramatic text.

The Teacher in Role

The work of Dorothy Heathcote has helped drama teachers to understand the functional significance of taking on a role. She makes clear that this implies much more than merely "joining in" and stresses that teachers in role must never act in the sense that an actor may, because they have a different job to do, a separate function.

The initial purpose of using role is emphatically *not* to give a display of acting, but to invite participants to enter the fictional world. Once this invitation has been accepted, participants can respond actively, begin to ask or answer questions, and oppose or transform what is taking place. The role presented by the teacher is available to be "read" publicly, and, like spectators at a play, the participants are entangled in a web of contemplation, speculation, and anticipation. Interest, commitment, and appropriate responses to what is being presented affirm the growth of group unity and identity. Participants are drawn together in attending to and building the event as they look for clues about the imagined world that is unfolding before them, as well as finding their place within it. They will be concerned to discover (from within) the action and the nature of the roles with which they have been endowed or have adopted, the relationships of these roles to that presented by the teacher, as well as the powers and functions that the rules of the game may permit them to acquire. Through the agency of the leader in role, and with the active cooperation of the participants, the dramatic world begins to define itself in action. If the leader functions merely as an extra, one of the crowd "adding to the number in the cast," the journey has begun, but there is still a long way to go.[5]

The advantages offered by working in role are manifold. These include initiating a piece of work through a dramatic and economic pretext, establishing atmosphere, modeling appropriate behaviors, moving the action forward, and challenging the participants from within. From inside the work, it is possible, as Brook notes, to "attack and yield, provoke and withdraw."[6] From the outside, it may appear that the leader is in complete control of the action, but the leader must also obey the developing logic of the piece and avoid arbitrary and individual decisions. The process is likely to work best when the leader permits the other participants to supply as many decisions as possible about content and restricts himself to finding a way to make these decisions into what Lin Wright has called "playable action."[7]

Mistaking the nature of their function, some leaders and teachers may decide to take on a role in the drama process in order to acquire control over it. Typically, the roles chosen under these circumstances may appear to possess the greatest authority—kings or queens, prison governors, ships' captains, the leaders of the explorers, and so on. Drama teachers sometimes fall into this error and attempt to subvert the drama to their own ends. Fortunately, children are often more expert at managing the rules and structures of dramatic play than are adults, and they know better. Kings can be replaced, prison governors killed, captains thrown overboard and leaders disobeyed. Such controlling teachers may be "dead" or disregarded within minutes of initiating the drama. The rules of the game permit their overthrow, as the children implicitly understand, and to join in the work implies that the teacher, too, must obey the rules. It will be necessary for leaders who fall into such traps to rethink their function and try to see *below* the surface power of the role.

Gavin Bolton claims that the practice of teacher in role challenges the very conception of teaching. He describes it both as a strategy for learning and a significant principle of teaching, one that uniquely inverts the assumptions underlying the traditional pedagogical context:

> The teacher in role has power but it is not of the conventional kind. It carries within it its opposite: a potential for being rendered powerless . . .The power relationship between pupils and teacher within the drama is tacitly perceived as negotiable.[8]

Spontaneity and Control

There are many implications for teachers or leaders who wish to work in this way from within the process. It will be important for them to change their modes of thinking and to alter their practice if they are to function effectively within the experience. It is not sufficient merely to create the right climate for experiment and to accept and encourage the spontaneity of the participants. Leaders must tolerate their own spontaneity as well. To be spontaneous does not imply behavior that is merely impulsive and unthinking. Spontaneity demands much more than this. It implies a quality of mind, the ability to think afresh, to balance impulse and restraint, and to integrate imagination, reason, and intuition.[9] Keith Johnstone describes the creative teacher as one who "gives permission" and reassures by example. This kind of leader will invite participants into the imagined world and support and protect them within it. Even willing participants need a teacher or leader who is living proof that imagination will not destroy them.[10]

Spontaneity also demands a certain generosity and freedom of spirit when submitting to the workings of a process that may not be entirely rational. This may not come easily to those who enjoy directorial control. Leaders in process drama must loosen their rational grip both on their own imagination and intuition and on the work itself. The integrity and autonomy of the work demands to be respected. The freedom to submit to the art object that we are shaping is one of the conditions of creativity.[11] Although it is realized through the presence of the participants, the work will develop an existence that is independent of them. If it does not in some sense take over, the process is likely to remain contrived and mechanical.

The difficulty presented by many otherwise useful handbooks on improvised drama is that the activities suggested may become scenarios, to be presented exactly as they are written, leaving little room for any real contribution from the participants. For example, in a drama session for elementary students about endangered species, the children are given information about the diminishing population of eagles and hear a story about the extinction of the carrier pigeon. They do preparatory movement exercises—breaking out of a shell, learning to fly—and listen to a song called "The Eagle and the Hawk." Next, they undertake a journey to meet the eagles.

> I can't see the mother. Oh no, she may have gone to find the father. But the babies may not hatch if she's gone for over a minute . . . Oh, she's back to the nest, and the father's flying above. I see him darting down. (Another shot is heard.) Oh, no . . . He's been killed. Do you still want to continue toward the nest? The mother has no help now to gather food. She has to remain on her nest. Do you think we could help her gather food?

The leader, or a child, puts on eagle's wings and a cap (made out of flannel) and delivers a monologue about the plight of the eagle. She thanks the children for their interest, which has given her new hope.

Although this is a worthy subject and the activities are probably enjoyable for the children, the treatment of the material presents problems. Genuine information about endangered eagles is mixed with fantasy—an invitation to find food for the eagle's babies. The session is very teacher-directed and allows little opportunity for the participants to take on roles, make decisions, and question assumptions. Educational and dramatic challenges are limited. Apart from a possible interaction with the leader in role as the eagle at the end of the session, the children seem to be required largely to follow the teacher's lead and be little more than an audience to the event.[12] It is important to remember that engagement in a dramatic world is always voluntary. Only participation in the creation of the dramatic world can bring that world into being, and in this example that participation is held to a minimum. The children are extras in the event, with no power to alter or control the action.

Leaders as Artists

For the artist, to work within the aesthetic process is an inevitable stance. In the theatre, the director, at least in this century, has been perceived as perhaps the most dominant artist in forging a performance. The leader or teacher who works in process drama will have to realign this more usual stance in order to function as an artist *within* the experience. It will not be enough to remain satisfied with providing what Witkin has called "the primary creative impulse" and placing participants "under starter's orders."[13]

Although process drama is a group process, it is no more democratic in its operation than is the production of a piece of theatre. The leader or teacher, working inside the creative process, may acquire some of the functions of the director, designer, stage manager, and even audience, but, because of the nature of the activity, will go beyond these purposes. The leader's primary tasks are those of managing the action, of operating the structure, and of functioning as a dramatist. The purpose is similar to that of the dramatist—to engage the participants in significant experience. Like the dramatist, the task for the leader who works through process drama is to alter at a stroke the participants' customary orientation to time and space. The aim is to lead them across the threshold of an imagined world, a world that comes into being as they enter it.

A drama world with its origin in an effective and resonant pre-text has the possibility of evolving organically according to a growing inner logic and coherence. As well as being shaped by the participants, it will also shape its creators. Submitting to the manipulation of the artwork is essential for the experience to take hold, and it also means that the participants adopt, at least for the purposes of the fictional world, the moral framework of the piece. The basis for any transformation of values is in part set up by the text.

This dramatic world and its moral framework is created and maintained by the efforts of everyone in the group, including the leader. Almost more sharply than theatre, these fictional worlds exploit the tensions between illusion and reality. Any illusions can only be established through the agreement of the group. Although I would argue that the leader has the primary responsibility for shaping the experience, ideally it will be the *work*—the creation and maintenance of the shared dramatic world—that dictates the ways in which it evolves. There is a kind of aesthetic necessity that begins to operate in the group process. Any creative structure will contain unknown variables, which must be accommodated. The artist works in a kind of open possibility, as does the leader in process drama.

> Like the scientific inquirer, the artist permits the subject-matter of his perception, in connection with the problems it presents, to determine the issue, instead of insisting upon its agreement with a conclusion decided in advance.[14]

The craftsperson uses skills to achieve a predetermined end, but the artist uses skills to discover ends through action.

Although the end of the work may not be known, each new stage will impose fresh choices and decisions that could not have been foreseen at an earlier stage. Utter watchfulness is the first necessity, an ability to be able to respond immediately to the innumerable variables that may enforce a subtle change of plan. Essential qualities in the leader or teacher are the toleration of anxiety and ambiguity, as well as a willingness to take risks and court mystery, and the courage to confront disappointment and, on occasion, the possibility of failure. These qualities must pervade the leader's approach to both the participants and the work, because the leader should both model and embody the attitudes that are integral to the creative endeavor. The leader or teacher will not *own* the work, although they may have done much to create it.

> If art, like nature, is a process, a continuing, changing event, and the artist a participant in nature, the artist is not one who makes special products but one who participates in the process.[15]

Each of the participants in process drama will be not just an actor, but also both playwright and spectator. Because the work is incomplete—in process—it will invite their participation at every level.

Ideally, the drama process will develop a life beyond its creators and the leader will become not the creator but a servant to the event, who labors to bring it into being. The task for the leader is to trap the participants in the confines of the dramatic world, as theatre workers do their audience, and then release them into the power of co-creation as dramatists, performers, and audience, so that the division between these functions is blurred and finally disappears.

The Liminal Servant

Peter McLaren, in a fascinating and provocative study, characterizes teachers as "liminal servants."[16] He borrows the concept of liminality from anthropology, and in particular from Victor Turner, who describes it as a social state, often an initiation or rite of passage in which participants lose their usual roles and status. Liminality defines a time and space "betwixt and between" one context of meaning and action and another. In this state, literally on the threshold (the "limen" in Latin), participants are neither what they have been or what they will be. They are caught up in a process of separation, transition, and transformation. This condition has close connections to playful and theatrical activities, which also belong to a time and space held apart from ordinary life.[17] For Richard Schechner, experimental theatre is liminal and exists like a cockroach in the "creases" of contemporary society. These creases provide places to hide, but they also signal areas of instability, disturbance, and potentially radical change.[18]

In the liminal state, people "play" with familiar elements and disarrange and defamiliarize them. Thus they are engaging in the basic activity of all art—defamiliarization—whose purpose, according to Shklovsky, is to impede perception, to force us to notice, to help us to see anew, to promote novel perspectives on the world.[19] McLaren regards every teacher, and in particular the teacher of drama, as a potential "liminal servant" whose duty is to engage in a kind of pedagogical surrealism that disturbs commonplace perceptions. This defamiliarization, which he sees as a crucial element in teaching and learning, relates closely to Brecht's "alienation effect" in theatre.

Both the drama teacher and the innovative theatre director are liminal servants. Working in role, the teacher can lead the students across the threshold into the imagined world of drama, a place of separation and transformation where the rules and relationships of classroom life are suspended. In this dramatic world, participants are free to alter their status, choose to adopt different roles and responsibilities, play with elements of reality, and explore alternate existences. When the dramatic world takes hold and acquires a life of its own, all of the participants will return across the threshold changed in some way, or at least not quite the same as when they began. As those who fear the power of art understand very clearly, if it is possible to imagine alternative realities, it is also possible to bring them into existence.

Guides without Maps

In recent years, the theatre director has been required to adopt increasingly complex functions and to operate at times almost as a psychiatrist, whose purpose is to free the actor from physical and emotional constraints. Peter Brook claims that the theatre director is "a guide at night who does not know the territory." Yet he has no choice, he must continue to guide, learning the route as he goes.[20] Leaders of process drama are also guides to new worlds, traveling with incomplete maps to the terrain, taking risks, and not knowing what lies ahead. I like to imagine these guides, the liminal servants to the work, trying to lead the way while walking backward, so that they do not become intent on reaching a predetermined destination as quickly as possible. It is as important for these guides to know the travelers' starting point, and the nature of the journey so far, as it is to determine the kind of journey that lies ahead. In process drama, the outcome of the journey is the journey itself. The experience is its own destination.

Transformations:
Roles and Roleplay

■ **Process drama** is closely aligned with contemporary theatre practice in its approach to role—that central feature of all theatre. The enacting of a role is as necessary to the theatre event as the living presence of the performer, because human behavior is its very subject. Theatre can occur without elaborations of setting, costumes, lighting, and even script, but its indispensable components are the living bodies of the actors and the actual presence of the onlookers.

In process drama the expressive means are usually limited, and the onlookers are also actors in the event, so it is primarily through their roles that participants create and maintain the dramatic world. During this extended experimental dramatic encounter, participants are likely to undertake multiple roles that require a simplicity of representation instead of complete identification and naturalistic portrayal. These roles are likely to be distinguished by an illustrative quality and will demand an ability to project into and respond to the ongoing dramatic situation. None of these factors will necessarily locate process drama outside the realm of theatre.

As soon as people consciously intend to be watched by others, they are engaging in acting behavior at some level and are perceived by others in an entirely new light. Their behavior has already become artificial and codified. This is true even of a person in plain view, whose appearance has not been altered by costume, make-up, or setting.

> [T]he actor's body is inscribed in a mechanism of meaning, which claims from the reluctant flesh its share of artificiality and codification.[1]

Actors undertaking a role become transparent, inviting the spectators to look through them at the character or, as in a mirror, at themselves.

Anyone who publicly takes on a fictional role becomes at once both more and less than an individual. The alteration in the interpretive attitude of the viewer modifies the status of the viewed. This is as true of the actor in a brief improvisation as it is of the hero of a classic drama. As soon as they are viewed in even the most vestigial role, actors acquire what Roland Barthes calls a "corporeal exemplarity."[2] Whether at the most developed end of the continuum of acting behavior or at the least personalized, actors represent different versions of humanity and will be recognized as types in the human family. However vague, nonnaturalistic, fragmented, or brief acting behavior may be, it will immediately be assigned a human significance by the watchers, because human presence and behavior are at the very heart of theatre. Indeed, it is possible to argue that the less individualized the role or character, the more the actor is likely to come to represent a type of humanity. In contemporary theatre, rather than aiming to embody a character as fully as possible, the actor often merely illustrates, suggests or presents a role. But at whatever level of elaboration or simplification, the actor's body is inevitably at the core of the theatre event, which is

> the site of an ultraincarnation, in which the body is double, at once a living body . . . and an emphatic, formal body, frozen by its function as an artificial object.[3]

Characterization and Simplification

Acceptable acting styles and types of representation will vary in every generation. In 1881, Zola longed for naturalism to triumph so that the stage could be rid of the actor as a mere symbol of vice or virtue, and people of flesh and bones could appear. He wanted characters to be determined by their environment and to act according to the logic of facts and the logic of their own dispositions.[4]

Less than ten years later, in the preface to *Miss Julie*, Strindberg wrote of creating his characters from "scraps of humanity, patched together like the human soul" in order to avoid the "bourgeois conception" of unchanging human nature.[5] Throughout the history of the drama, the actor has always embodied changing concepts of humanity.

Acting has been undergoing a gradual process of simplification throughout the twentieth century, and this process can be traced to developments in performance theory and playwriting as well as to a growth in our psychological understanding. These changes are part of a cyclical process of evolution from the actor as the personifier of an abstraction, as in *Everyman* and other morality plays, to the actor as impersonator in naturalistic drama, to the actor as a depersonalized element in avant-garde theatre. In postmodern drama, even the individualized human subject begins to disappear. There is an emphasis on body and image rather than on character.

In conventional theatre, the notion of effective characterization in acting has been influenced profoundly by ideas of character more suited to the novel, the dominant literary form of the nineteenth century. A significant change in the drama—from depicting a metaphysical reality to portraying the inner reality of individual experience—has emerged since the end of the seventeenth century.

Because the drama was limited to expressing inner experience through human action, it began to be replaced by the novel, which could more fully convey an inner world. The development of the notion of the "round" character behaving with the complexity and incalculability of life, whose thoughts, emotions, and motivations are made available to us by the omniscience of the novelist, parallels that of psychology. Much of this organization is not available to the dramatist, nor is it necessarily desirable. It is important to remember that psychology is merely a byproduct of the drama and not its true life. Psychology itself has changed in recent decades. Personality is no longer seen as a self-contained entity, but as a process of growth, interaction, and transformation.

Character as Function

Every trait displayed by a character in a play is significant only in its effect. Its relevance is not primarily as an elaboration of character but as an event in the plot. Characterization depends on function. Ricoeur has provided a useful definition of *function* as an act of a character defined from the point of view of its significance for the course of the action.[6] Dramatic characters define themselves through their behaviors and interactions, as well as in what is said of them by others. Definition of character in drama means a display of those personal traits and aspects of personal history that are relevant to the dramatist's purpose and the omission of all extraneous detail. It is not possible merely to divide characters into those that seem lifelike and those that are instantly recognizable as "stock" types. All lifelike characters owe their consistency to the appropriateness for their dramatic function of the stock type on which they are based. That stock type is not the character, but is as necessary to the character as is the skeleton to the actor playing the part. Because dramatic characters are defined precisely by their context, it is inevitable that they will partake, to some degree, of the nature of types and may even remain "stereotype figures and theatrical scarecrows," as Thomas Mann called them. Mann regarded drama as the art of the silhouette. The novel, for him, was always

> more precise, more complete, more knowing, conscientious and profound in everything that concerns our insight into the body and soul of man . . . narrative is the only true, complete, round and three-dimensional channel for presenting mankind in literature.[7]

In performance, of course, the dramatic character is actually physically present before us in disturbing corporeality, already three-dimensional in a way that no novel could hope to emulate. The fragmentary nature of dramatic characterization may in fact more closely resemble our real-life knowledge of other people than the fullness of insight that is possible to acquire from a novel. The overemphasis by earlier critics on character analysis has been balanced in recent years by a less "psychological" approach that does not regard dramatic characters as "historical" or real figures.

The weakness of much modern American drama has been identified as a tendency to make character everything and action nothing. The simple belief that character is best pursued in the absence of action may lead to a commitment to stasis.

> To observe life carefully, you must make it stand still. To make life stand still, you must deal with the stillborn—characters unable to change themselves, their relationships, or the world about them.[8]

An emphasis on character is likely to mean that the actors are sunk in what Michel Saint Denis called "the mud of naturalism," although in contemporary drama this mud may be overlaid by apparently nonnaturalistic elements.[9] For example, Brian Friel's acclaimed play *Dancing at Lughnasa* is introduced and interrupted by a narrator, who is simultaneously an adult actor addressing the audience directly and an invisible presence in the action as a seven-year-old boy. Despite this dislocation of perception, the play remains almost Chekhovian in its effect. The play finally achieves an effect that comes perilously close to less ambitious and popular "family photograph album" plays such as *Brighton Beach Memoirs, I Remember*

Mama, and *A Voyage Round My Father.* Although brief outbursts of joy and energy enliven the play, there is a static, elegiac quality common to this kind of theatre, and insufficient rediscovery, interrogation, or reinterpretation of that past, which is ostensibly the play's subject. Friel's five Irish sisters, however, whose lives are defined by narrowness and lack of opportunity, are characterized in satisfying dramatic detail.

Illusion and Transformation

"Childish attempts to be real" have been replaced by a recognition that all acting is, by definition, unreal.[10] There is nothing more illusory in performance than the illusion of actuality, particularly the fallacy of a unity of character. The task for the actor will always be something more than the mere attempt to imitate life in a realistic and detailed fashion. It is primarily the actor who defines the level of reality at which the spectator places the action on the stage. This can be done by a direct appeal to the audience ("Let's pretend"), an elaborate disregard of the audience ("This is an alternative reality"), or, as in some improvised drama, involvement with the audience ("Let's make a new reality together"). Each different version of reality is always an exercise in illusion, dependent for its success on the contract established between actors and audience. The level of "reality" of the theatre event is selected and maintained by the attitude of the performers both to the characters in the play and to the audience.[11]

Since Brecht, playwrights have realized many possibilities other than merely submerging the actor in the role. To observe someone acting, for Sartre, is to encounter a person "devoured by the imaginary."[12] This phrase suggests a kind of total submission to the demands of the imagined world, which is no longer regarded as essential in contemporary theatre. The possibilities offered by highlighting the "unreal" nature of acting have increasingly been explored and exploited. Grotowski, following Artaud, proposed that the actors should transform themselves before the spectator's eyes and claimed that the magic of theatre consists in seeing this transformation as it comes to birth.[13] In his work, the spectators encounter the actor as a person who is not so much a character in the play as the subject of the play. Improvisation, which thrives on role changes and transformations, has been an important factor in this movement away from the naturalistic portrayal of character. Many innovative directors want their audiences to feel the direct experience of the actors as well as the characters they portray. Actors are no longer required to submerge themselves in the roles they represent but may be encouraged to regard themselves as part of a community that includes the audience. To emphasize this connection, the audience may be permitted to observe the actors in the process of transforming themselves into the characters. Actors may be in character one minute and out of character the next.

Making visible the actor's movement into role is an important part of the purpose of Mike Alfreds, founder and director of the company Shared Experience, who sees these transformations as the necessary heart of theatre. In Alfreds' work, the actor visibly transforms himself in the presence of his audience, and the audience experiences the transformation simultaneously with the actor, shares this act of imagination, and is made vividly aware of its essential duality.[14] The theatrical excitement generated by these visible transformations was demonstrated by the critical and popular acclaim that greeted the Royal Shakespeare Company's *Nicholas Nickleby,* in which leading actors appeared in a succession of roles of varying importance and contrasting effect. At times, the actors also collectively played inanimate objects (the coach, for example), as well as presented emotions or ideas rather than characters. Performances of this kind achieve their effects by working *against* the magic of illusion.

These transformations and the expansion of the possibilities of role are well established in process drama, where a role may be played by a single person or by everyone in the group simultaneously or consecutively, and where abstract ideas or feelings may be presented or interpreted (for example, in the use of tableaux). Characters in process drama tend, by the nature of the activity, to be members of a particular group, and this group orientation provides their initial perspective on the unfolding dramatic event. Their individual identities are necessarily more fluid and less predictable than those of characters minutely defined in advance. The relationship between the participants and the different roles they adopt in the drama is flexible.

In much avant-garde theatre, acting tends to the physical and pictorial and may not necessarily demand any virtuosity or advanced technique. Actors no longer separate themselves from the audience by any obviously trained or artificial manner of speech or bearing. This development can be seen as part of a process of the emancipation of the actor from the domination of the playwright, the director, and eventually even the role and the character. The ultimate end of the process of depersonalized acting is where actors find themselves without character, role, or theme—required to improvise an entire performance.

Doubling

This shift away from the presentation of the fully rounded character on stage has not been entirely ideological and artistic. In recent years it seems to have become popular, at least in part because of financial constraints. The financial pressure on theatre companies to use as few actors as possible has meant that audiences have come to accept and applaud the "doubling" of characters, even in commercial plays. Thus, advances in technique have grown from the effort to solve both commercial and artistic problems.

Instead of attempting to obscure this doubling of roles, playwrights and directors may deliberately exploit the situation. Doubling can become a virtue, displaying the virtuosity of the performers, heightening the awareness of theatricality, and inevitably calling attention to the theatrical process itself. Serious drama always includes a dimension of the metadramatic and encompasses the essential dramatic theme of human perception.

Doubling was used to great effect in *Our Country's Good,* a powerfully metadramatic piece that had its premiere at the Royal Court Theatre in London in 1988. A small, multiracial company played officers, soldiers, and male and female convicts putting on Farquhar's *Recruiting Officer* during the first year of the settlement in Australia. One of the female convicts is eager to play Sergeant Kite. When she is told that this will be unacceptable to the spectators (who have already seen women doubling as officers, as well as the character Sylvia disguised as a soldier in the play within the play), she insists that "People with no imaginations shouldn't go to the theatre."[15] This is a highly charged metatheatrical moment, both collaborative and self-referential, in which actors and audience share their explicit understanding of the double pretense of theatre. Such direct applications of drama to life afford significant and manifold perspectives on both the world of the play and the world surrounding it. Both the play and the play within the play become an examination of the power of theatre to explore alternative identities, capacities, and possibilities. The artificial boundaries of the play open out to include our own world. Mainstream theatre is inevitably affected by these innovations. In London, the successful commercial production of *Travels with my Aunt,* an adaptation of Grahame Greene's novel, used four actors who take turns playing the Aunt, as well as sharing all the other parts. Performances of this kind achieve their effects precisely by working against the magic of illusion. They also educate the mainstream audience to accept a broader range of styles, conventions, and possibilities.

Identification and Projection

Actors doubling and switching among roles will also affect the spectators' engagement with the event. A useful outcome is that their habit of confusing the actor with the character can be challenged. Identification with the leading character is no longer possible under these circumstances and indeed has always been a somewhat doubtful concept. We might expect to identify most closely with the most fully realized characters, the "great" characters of dramatic literature. But these towering figures, the Heddas and Hamlets, always retain something mysterious and elusive at their core. They hold us to some degree at a distance, as they do the characters by whom they are surrounded in the play. It is this quality that is the secret of their continuing hold on the imaginations of performers and audiences alike.

Identification in theatre is not at all similar to the kinds of identification available to the reader of novels. In the novel, as well as possessing an intimate knowledge of the protagonists' thoughts and feelings, we are free to visualize their physical appearances and may endow them with qualities that are reflections of the way we perceive ourselves. In theatre the characters are present before our eyes, clearly set apart from us and embodied in particular human presences as both individuals and types. But although they have their own separate being, the protagonists on stage will always, to some degree, exemplify us. By virtue of appearing before us, actors represent us, stand in for us, and embody a type of humanity as much as an individual. It is always ourselves we see on the stage. This endowment of character will occur in the absence of a script and even if the actor says or does nothing. Immobility itself will become charged with significance as we struggle to make human meaning and sense from what we see before us.

It would appear that our powers of identification are actually increased when the protagonists are not too sharply characterized, apart from their most essential elements. As soon as characterization and detail are increased, we are likely to respond as critics rather than as participants.

> Characterization in a play is like a blank check which the dramatist accords to the actor for him to fill in—not entirely blank, for a number of indications of individuality are already there, but to a far less definite degree than in the novel.[16]

The playwright David Mamet agrees that the wise actor will not work too hard to fill in all the blanks. He believes that it is the strength to avoid over-elaboration and to resist the extraneous that renders acting both powerful and beautiful.[17] All great drama will work best by leaving much of the endowment of characters, place, and action to the audience. It is for the same reason that a half-completed stage design can be so much more effective and evocative in the theatre than a detailed realistic setting or the introduction of real items onto the stage.

Both the necessity and the possibility of fully realized dramatic characters is a notion that has been questioned continuously. In farce or realistic drama, there may be a completeness of design or a straightforwardness of character, but these details are needed in order to locate the action precisely in its specific social setting. Interestingly, for Yeats, character was continuously present in comedy alone, where the social setting and relationships are necessarily more specific and precise. In tragedy, he believed that the idea of character was often replaced by externally declared and displayed passions and emotions.[18]

In the theatre, a degree of identification or empathy may be at work in the audience, although empathy has been defined as an almost purely physical response. A more useful concept, especially when considering this phenomenon in process drama, may be that of projection. There may be a gradual increase of involvement for the audience from projection through identification to empathy. I believe that these phases of commitment also may be applicable to the different levels of participation in process drama. These levels move from a generalized involvement, through more detailed engagement, to the kind of dynamic participation that is both active and reflective.

In our responses to a theatre event, we project *into* the situation rather than identify with single characters and their fate. If there is identification, it is with the entire situation rather than with some selected character or with certain events. For Brecht, too complete an identification of the spectators with what was happening on the stage was essentially disabling, but even his attempts at disruption and distance and his emphasis on the structure of appearances and the historical *gestus* does not entirely preclude an active projection by the spectators into the situations he sets before them. Stanislavski required his actors to transform themselves into the selves of the characters they played, while the Brechtian actor was distanced from the role, and "demonstrated" rather than "impersonated" the characters and their worlds, in order to promote a kind of objectivity in the spectator. Hornby noted that although this is apparently the opposite of the Stanislavski/Method approach, there is an underlying similarity, because in both cases the actor's ego boundary remains intact. The Stanislavski approach places the performance inside that boundary, the Brechtian approach places it outside, but the boundary—the actor's sense of her everyday self—does not change. Both types of actor, in Hornby's view, are finding ways to avoid acting.[19]

Different acting styles lead to different kinds of theatre. Different types of theatre, in turn, alter the actor's role-acquisition strategies and even those of the spectators. Avant-garde ensembles are interested in investigating the actor-audience relationship and often attempt to involve the spectators in roleplaying or to endow them with roles and attitudes. The reluctance of some audience members to accept these roles demonstrates their capacity to retain considerable autonomy over the level of their engagement in the theatre event and to reject what they do not regard as appropriate involvement.

Acting and Roleplay

"Acting" as a description of the work drama teachers undertake with students has been a rather unpopular one. For their purposes, the term may carry implications of conspicuous theatrical and exhibitionistic qualities that are both irrelevant and destructive to their educational purposes. The term *roleplay* has been preferred in the classroom and drama studio, although both acting and roleplay require the same basic ability to project into a variety of fictional situations by pretending to be someone or something other than one's self. The simplicity and immediacy with which this ability can be exercised in process drama have led some commentators to see it as less developed or worthwhile, as somehow lower in the hierarchy of acting behavior than that requiring detailed rehearsal and characterization.

Drama lessons and workshops often include activities that are not easily translated into imagined worlds or dramatic characters, for example, trust games and concentration exercises. Drama teachers have sometimes found it useful to employ the terms *roleplay* or *role drama* to indicate that part of their work that has to do with the creation of fictional roles and situations. Roleplay carries both the implication of a functional quality as well as an instrumental and didactic purpose. In these cases, role is primarily defined by its function, and its instrumental purpose is based on the fact that as well as implying particular behaviors, roles can be seen as "inescapable mechanisms" for coping with the business of living in the world.[20] Roleplay allows these "mechanisms" to be practiced in safety, but it is important to realize that practicing particular social roles may actually reaffirm them. Instead of enlarging role possibilities for the participants or encouraging them to challenge the roles that society expects them to undertake, functional roleplay may work eventually to confirm students in the restricted range of roles most readily available to them in the world. This is a denial of an essential function of theatre, which is to enhance our sense of ourselves and to reaffirm the multiple existential potentialities we incorporate but cannot always realize.

People in occupational roles are "playing" with their condition in order to realize it and perform it effectively in public, according to Sartre.

> There are indeed many precautions to imprison a man in what he is, as if we lived in perpetual fear that he might escape from it, that he might break away and elude his condition.[21]

Once we move beyond the limited confines of functional roleplay, both theatre and improvisation allow us to "elude our condition," to perform our "unacted part."[22] In fact, they motivate us to do so. Nothing interests us more than ourselves and our potentialities. Camus provided a vivid image of the actor as a traveler in time, a hunted traveler who is pursued by the souls of characters yearning to possess him.[23] The whole concept of theatre is founded on the construction of possible selves and of alternative realities, and dramatic activity is the direct result of our ability to play with and transform the roles we inhabit. Theatre is an innovative laboratory for the exercise of our capacity to transcend the social roles and types that in real life we may have been unable to elude. It is our potential selves and the self that is audience to our own performances that calls every kind of theatre into being.

Aspects of Role

Moreno, in his pioneering use of role in therapy and training, defined roleplaying as the personification of other forms of existence through the medium of play.[24] He saw it as a technique, not just for practicing existing roles, but for the exploration and expansion of the self into an unknown universe. Spontaneity and creativity were central to this process. Moreno distinguished two major manifestations of role. The first was *role taking,* the enactment of a situation in a totally predetermined manner. The second he called *role creating,* which involves a spontaneous response appropriate to the given circumstances. It is this spontaneity that is at the heart of the roles that arise in improvised drama.

For Dorothy Heathcote, taking on a role means that there is a need to "read" the situation, to harness relevant information from previous experience, and to realign this information so that new understanding becomes possible. Like Moreno, she believes that the most important aspect of taking on a role is its spontaneity. It is unplanned, unpremeditated, and as a result can constantly surprise the individual into new awareness. She stresses that children should not be asked to act in the "stage actor sense," only that they should take up attitudes and perspectives, and for the time operate within them.[25] This is close to the demonstrative and illustrative quality expected of a Brechtian actor.

In roleplay, the roles undertaken are defined and recognized by their functions. Taking on roles will illuminate and exhibit these functions. Sometimes what seems to be required of participants in much classroom roleplay is not that they should begin to act, but that they remain themselves, even when adopting roles and functioning in whatever way the fictional situation demands of them. As O'Toole puts it, under these circumstances the participants are enrolled in the drama as "themselves," and are expected to behave as themselves, but in ways that are appropriate to the situation.[26] They may be asked to do little more than adapt functionally to the situation of the drama in much the same way as they might adapt to the functions required in a game. This approach is essentially limiting, and a denial of the possibilities of the medium.

Bolton stresses that however functional a role may be, it will still need to be performed.[27] Roleplaying can be received, affirmed, and validated by others in the group only through this outward performance. Appearance is universal to any kind of performance, however basic. Without this public dimension—the embodiment and display—any kind of roleplay will remain at the level of fantasy. It is through our encounters with others that we affirm our sense of self in the real world, and the same is true in the imagined world of process drama. Even the most limited and functional kind of role taking will demand some degree of self-transcendence, something that goes beyond the actual here and now. Participants in roleplay are simultaneously an audience to their own acts and observers of the consequences of these acts. Their understanding of human behavior is objectified through language and gesture and is available for both reconstruction and reflection. In enactment that has an intrinsic purpose, roleplaying will be undertaken for its own sake. It is a collaboration, a disinterested experiment into the making of possible selves. Through theatre and process drama we can reinvent ourselves, discover what we may be, and live in what Heathcote calls the "no-penalty zone" of these powers and possibilities.[28]

Modeling and Managing

Bolton regards *dramatic playing,* his term for the improvisational mode in process drama, as only one instance of an event that requires the participants to enter into a contract to create it, and he believes that the kind of "acting behavior" demanded by the event is qualitatively no different from that used in adjusting to different social events and contexts. Drawing on the work of ethnomethodologists, he has distinguished between "modeling" behavior, which is used to reproduce or represent an external reality, and "managing" behavior, which responds existentially to the reality that is "here and now." The first kind of acting—modeling behavior—resembles the activity of the actor, whose representation of a character in a play can be prepared beforehand and is expected to conform to what is set down in the script. In the latter, where participants are managing the unfolding dramatic action, role function will provide "a minimal relational starting point," and characterization will be only significant retrospectively.[29]

Although participants in process drama are likely to engage in acting behavior that is fairly simplified, different kinds of engagement in the imagined world may be required of them. Morgan and Saxton list five "categories of identification" to define the levels at which participants are likely to operate.[30] These are

1. Dramatic playing: being oneself in a make-believe situation.
2. Mantle of the Expert: being oneself but looking at the situation from a particular point of view.
3. Roleplaying: representing an attitude or point of view.
4. Characterizing: representing an individual lifestyle, which may be different from that of the participant.
5. Acting: selecting movement, gesture, and voice to represent a particular individual to others.

This is a useful list, revealing the influence of Heathcote's work, but categories of acting may not be defined so easily in practice. Even those who may be operating at levels 1, 2, or 3 are likely to use movement, gesture, and voice to represent the fictional role or situation to others in the group. There is an implied hierarchy in the list, but engagement in process drama may require participants to shift among these categories. Depending on the challenges presented by the imagined world, level 5 may not necessarily be more demanding than level 1. The temptation for the participant in improvised drama is to adopt a kind of clichéd acting behavior that remains, in Bolton's terms, a "modeling" activity, repeating easily recognizable stereotypes. Such clichés may seem helpful at first in the high-risk world of improvisation, but when energy is spent on maintaining these cliches, no discoveries are possible. If these roles are not capable of being mediated and articulated, the work is likely to remain superficial and banal.

Concealment and Disclosure

The essential requirements for the role in process drama are the same as for the character in a classic play. To play a role rather than a character is not necessarily a limited or limiting activity. The roles that occur in process drama will acquire complexity in precisely the same way that the characters in plays acquire it. Action must be undertaken that will reveal the true nature of the role and begin to answer the question, "Who is this who is here?" Dramatic language is distinguished by the fact that it will always carry more meaning than its obvious surface intentions. All of the lines spoken on stage, among their other purposes, are disclosures of identity. This disclosure is at the heart of theatre, and, paradoxically, is achieved most effectively through a prolonged concealment. Because the theatre is essentially a public medium, a spectacle—the tension between what is evident and what is secret, concealed, or disguised—provides an essential source of dramatic power.

It is difficult to think of a play of any stature in which there is not a hidden identity, literal or metaphorical, that eventually comes to light. I believe that identity and the questions it raises are fundamental themes of all drama and therefore, by extension, of process drama. The way in which this theme is most often explored is not just through acting alone but through acting and roleplaying—in other words, through roleplaying within the role.

Roleplaying Within the Role

To act means not only to engage in an action, but also to impersonate. Actors performing the part of Hamlet or Iago are engaging in impersonation, but so are Hamlet and Iago. Is honest Iago honest, or is Hamlet really mad? These characters are also acting, or roleplaying.

They are repeating the basic dramatic situation of the actor, pretending to be something they are not. The most powerful way in which even the simplest and most functional role can acquire complexity is that which dramatists have used throughout the ages—to require their characters to roleplay within their roles. The audience sees a person pretending to be a certain kind of person who is pretending to be another kind of person. The pretense is doubled or even tripled. In *As You Like It,* Rosalind, played by a boy in Shakespeare's day, is pretending to be a girl who is pretending to be a boy, who roleplays a girl at certain moments. In the light of the definition of roleplay as a teaching tool, it is intriguing that this final roleplay is undertaken for educational purposes—to instruct Orlando about love. Here, as often happens, the audience is an accomplice in the conspiracy of disguise, but on occasion, as in Jonson's *Epicoene,* the spectators are also deceived. Like the characters in the play, they also learn the lesson of the deceptiveness of appearances, and the experience of the play extends out into the world of the audience.

As spectators, we are not confused by double or even triple impersonations. Instead, our powers of discrimination are sharpened by them. After all, that is the purpose of these impersonations. Attention is focused on the attributes of the various roles presented to us and the success with which the characters carry out their role functions, and we become adept at recognizing the qualities, characteristics, and truth of each. Many of the roles that characters find themselves required to play actually contradict, complicate, or deny their original roles: false friends, smiling villains, timid playboys, bourgeois gentlemen, ignoble kings, respectable prostitutes, earthy saints. Through the operation of these double roles, we encounter paradox in action.

As soon as there is roleplaying within the role, the theatre audience or the participants in process drama have a precise task to engage and focus their attention. This task is to discover the truth of the situation unfolding before them. It involves judgement and discrimination, detection and interpretation. As part of a theatre audience or as participants in process drama, we are in a privileged position. We see the truth of the situation more clearly than the actors, or at least we struggle to do so. We watch the mask of appearance, but we are aware of the reality behind it. We know the tension between the inside and the outside of the situation. We search for meaning in the appearances before us. We seek, like the Duke in *Measure for Measure,* to discover "what these seemers be." The interactions and encounters that develop will therefore have a built-in structure, an essentially dra-

matic tension, and as a result are likely to avoid the slackness and banality of many improvisations. There is much more to be discovered
about the nature and functions of role from working in this multilay-
ered mode than in any amount of one-dimensional roleplay.

Bolton points out that there are always constraints on the expression of crude conflict or emotion and "a withholding, a deceiving, a
restraining" in this kind of activity.[31] I believe that although other constraints—of time, task, or location, for example—may be useful and
effective, the single most powerful dramatic constraint in both theatre and process drama is the kind of concealment and disguise offered by roleplaying within the role. It is precisely here that the
double nature of theatre is most clearly at work. Playing a role is the
means by which the very concept of role itself is investigated. In all
kinds of drama, roleplay is both the medium and the message.

Roleplaying within the role, dissimulation, disguise, deception,
and concealment are everywhere in theatre.[32] They are not the special province of tragedy or comedy. Comedy thrives on disguise, mistaken identity, concealment, and deception. Consider *She Stoops to
Conquer, Tartuffe, The Importance of Being Earnest, The Playboy of
the Western World,* and *Twelfth Night.* This concealment is at the very
heart of farce, as well as providing the motivating force for the greatest tragedies. Disguise and confusions of identity are more than
mere stage conventions or devices. They are deeply structural and
cross different genres and eras of theatre history. One of the most
effective and amusing incidents in the Wakefield Mystery Plays is
Mac the Sheepstealer's attempt to prove that the stolen sheep hidden
in the cradle is, in fact, his baby. Appearances are being manipulated,
as they are by Edmund, Edgar, Kent, and the daughters in *King Lear*
or the brothers in Schiller's *The Robbers.* Like all enduring dramas,
these plays are founded on disguises, concealments, and deceptions.
Even their titles may hint at ambiguity, paradox, and pretense—for
example, *The White Devil* and *The Changeling.*

It is not only the other characters or the audience who are the victims of concealment or deception. Often we see characters who have
spent their lives deceiving themselves, denying their roles or creating
fictional worlds within worlds into which they can escape—in *Richard
II, Life's a Dream, The Bourgeois Gentilhomme, Death of a Salesman,
Who's Afraid of Virginia Woolf, Billy Liar, The Glass Menagerie, A
Streetcar Named Desire,* and almost all of Chekhov's plays. Identity, for
the characters in these plays, becomes associated with a struggle with
a given role, and more particularly with its denial or its loss.[33]

Watching other people take on a role, or adopting a role oneself, is always accompanied by a sense of ambivalence. Although it is the most "real" item present, the duplicity of the actor's body is much more profound than the painted sets and fake furniture of the stage.[34] When we role-play, we are transformed into something we are not, and then, by multiplying the number of roles we undertake, we are transformed again. Paradoxically, the real purposes of our roles will be revealed by attempts to disguise or deny them.

Like theatre, process drama gains in power and complexity by exploiting the tensions between appearance and reality, mask and face, and role and identity that lie at the heart of the theatrical experience. Even when the role within the original role is obviously false or limited, this dualistic device will give rise inevitably to a sense of complexity, feelings of ambivalence, and language that is both ambiguous and ironic in its effect. In contemporary theatre, the actor can be seen as

> a symbol of a permanent negotiation and re-negotiation between the determinism of roles and the existential freedom of each player.[35]

In process drama, this negotiation is at the very heart of the activity.

Role in Process Drama

All of these transformations and the expansion of the possibilities of role are well established in process drama, where a role may also be played by a single person or by everyone in the group simultaneously or consecutively, and where abstract ideas or feelings may be presented for contemplation and interpretation. Characters in process drama tend, by the nature of the activity, to be defined initially by their roles as members of a particular group involved in a specific enterprise or circumstance—for example, as townspeople, journalists, psychiatrists, celebrities, or advisers, according to the demands of the dramatic situation. This group orientation provides their initial perspective on the unfolding dramatic event and is likely to have a distancing effect. Their individual identities are necessarily less static and predictable than those of characters minutely defined in advance, but this flexibility permits genuine responses to the dramatic encounter within the logic of the situation. There is a need for each participant to "read" and monitor the appropriateness of her own engagement in the drama as it unfolds.

The Seal Wife

Examples of the multiple roles available to the participants in process drama can be traced in a session based on an Irish folktale, *The Seal Wife*. In this extended workshop with Australian drama educators, which lasted over two days, the participants engaged in acting behavior at a variety of levels, from illustrating and embodying characters in the story, to representing disembodied voices and natural forces, to improvising naturalistically, to being audience to the event.

The story that provided the pre-text for the work goes as follows:

For three nights, a young fisherman, Patrick, watches a beautiful woman sitting on the seashore and sees her don a skin and become a seal. He steals her skin and she is forced to return to his cottage and become his wife. They have three children. Seven years later, the thatch of their cottage is being renewed, and the thatchers throw down the sealskin from where the fisherman has hidden it. The children run with it to their mother. That night, she steals out of the house while they are sleeping, goes down to the shore, puts on the sealskin, and returns to the sea forever.

Episodes	Drama Elements
The first task for the participants was to create in small groups a tableau of one moment from the seven years during which the seal wife lived with the fisherman and bore him three children.	In these **tableaux**, which are composed rather than improvised, the group members represent the characters in the story, but also objects and elements—for example, the sea.
The second task for the group required each participant who represented the fisherman in the tableaux to form a new image, a continuum, showing Patrick at different stages of his life.	In this continuum, each actor illustrates a version of Patrick, but these remain representations rather than roles, with six different embodiments of the fisherman available for **contemplation** and **interpretation** by the group.
The next step is to locate these strange happenings in a specific world. Each person in the group becomes a member of the community in which the story takes place, and each has an attitude to or an opinion about the seal wife. They walk about and whisper their opinions and rumors to everyone else.	Here, each participant represents an attitude, a point of view, which determines what they say. The leader orchestrates their whisperings so that voices rise and fall in a chorus of suspicion and alienation.

Everyone chooses a partner. One person in each pair is asked to take on the role of either the seal wife or the fisherman and remain as audience to the next activity. The others become schoolchildren and sit on the floor with the leader, who takes on the role of the teacher in the village school. The teacher gives the children a task. As part of a class project on the sea, they must ask their parents to tell them tales and legends about the sea.

Two roles are shared among the whole group. For the first time, roles are improvised naturalistically, and yet half the group are cast as the seal-wife's children. This apparent illogicality does not prevent powerful projection into these roles. There is a strong subtext, because both children and parents know that they will be required to discuss forbidden subjects. Already, there is a pressure of concealment and possible disclosure.

The participants in role as children return to their parents and ask them to tell them what they know about the sea.

The encounter between the two participants is improvised **naturalistically**. There is no audience to this episode, and the participants are free to explore their responses.

The children, again at school, retell what their mothers have told them of the sea, but not naturalistically, more as a collage of voices, speaking as and when they wish.

It is worth noting that this sharing of fragments of the previous interaction has a strong sense of **audience**, provided by the parents, who are hearing their words retold.

Working in two large groups, the participants create a dream sequence. One dream is the fisherman's and the other is the seal wife's. Movement, speech, and sound are distorted and fragmented. Each group presents its dream to the other as **audience**.

Here, characters in the story are embodied by the group, as well as objects such as nets and boats, and natural elements like the wind and the waves. Much of the same imagery of loss and longing occurs in each **dream.**

Working individually, everyone writes a short poem or letter, responding to what they have experienced in the work so far.

Each person can choose a particular perspective from which to write— seal wife, fisherman, child, detached observer, or commentator.

After a break, the feeling level of the work is reestablished through a game. The participants work in pairs and, with their eyes shut, get to know each other's hands. Then

This is a **game** of seeking and finding and of loss and rejection. It can have a powerful emotional effect. Some participants clearly project strongly into their roles as they search for their true partner.

they separate and move about, still
blind, trying to identify their
partner's hands from among all of
the people in the group.

The work so far has been within the timeframe of the original story. The
leader narrates an introduction to the next phase. Ten years have passed
since the seal wife returned to the sea. The eldest child has fallen in love
and has a need to know more about the relationship between her parents.
Out of role, the participants, using a Forum Theatre approach, negotiate
the opening of a scene between Patrick and his daughter.

Two of the participants volunteer to
take on the roles of father and
daughter. The location of the scene
and the opening lines are negotiated by the group. The daughter
asks, "When did my mother first
fall in love with you?" The rest of
the scene is improvised, with the
onlookers offering suggestions.

Here, for the first time, the roles
have been **cast**, and are being embodied by particular participants,
yet the encounter is being moni-
tored and to some degree structured by the observers, who,
because of their previous involvement, have a considerable stake in
the enterprise.

Working in groups of six, each participant contributes one line to the
dialogue between father and daughter. No one is allowed to read anyone
else's line until all have been written.

This way of generating a kind of
random text has an initially **distancing** effect, requiring participants to limit their input.

Groups exchange their six-line
scripts and choose actors to play
out these scripts. They direct the
actors in order to make sense of
the lines and develop varying interpretations. The interactions between the father and daughter are
quite intense.

Participants are now working tech-
nically, considering how to stage
their **scripts** effectively. Only the
actors chosen in each group have
the opportunity to project into the
role. The challenge is to make
meaning from these random texts,
changing them as little as possible
in the process.

Because the previous activity has been rather cerebral, a change of pace is
needed. The leader narrates the next part of the work. Generations have
passed since the events in the story. The only traces of the legend that remain in the community are enshrined in a folkdance.

Working in two large groups, the
participants create a **folkdance**.

This physical activity has a
celebratory quality, but also reflects

Some elements of the dance mirror the events of the folktale, but are simplified and distorted. Each group shares their dance with the other group.

on the previous experiences of the drama. Roles are minimal and are diffused among the dancers.

There is still a sense of something unfinished in the work. The leader invites anyone in the group who has projected strongly into the role of the fisherman during the drama, either physically or mentally, to volunteer for the next activity. Six of the group do so, and sit isolated throughout the room with their eyes closed. They are given permission to abandon their roles at any point if they are uncomfortable. The rest of the participants circle around them, and whisper to them as the **voices** of the seal wife or her children.

This is a highly fraught activity for the those who have accepted the roles of the fisherman. Although they are not required to respond in any way, their immobility means that they are receptive to the voices of the others—often accusatory, longing, and full of pain. For each of the fishermen this was a powerful and often painful experience. Some time for reflection among those who had taken on the roles of the fisherman was needed here to deal with the feelings that arose.

As a final activity, each person chose one of the poems and letters written earlier, but not their own. They then chose what they thought was the most powerful and moving word, phrase, or sentence from the piece. Standing all together, they read their fragments, piecing them together without previous planning or editing. This new **text** was a further reflection on the events of the story and on the text generated in action by the participants.

Throughout this extended piece of work, there was no conventional or consistent acting or roleplaying of particular characters. Instead, all of the participants were engaged with the events of the story and their implications for the characters. They were at times involved and at times detached, and the different fragments of improvised, composed, and scripted projections into the event came together in a mosaic of meaning. The lack of specific and continuous identification with a single character did not prevent meanings, interpretations, and feelings being generated and investigated. The nature of the relationship between the husband and wife was the subject of particular scrutiny, as degrees of guilt and blame for the forced marriage were explored. These explorations were supported by the fact that the pre-text, the story of the seal wife, was centrally concerned with the concealment and denial or repression of a true identity, and the imposition and final rejection of traditional role expectations.

This same pre-text was the source of our process drama when I worked on a reservation in northern Manitoba with a group of Cree Indian highschool students. Their work developed differently over a shorter time, but they also became the seal wife's family and the gossiping members of the community. Finally they took on the roles of a kind of High Council of animal spirits and considered the request of the seal wife to return to her human family once more. They doubted the wisdom of this, but finally agreed and sent the Raven with her for wisdom and protection, and the Mouse for comfort. The differences in the culture and heritage of these two groups led to the exploration of a range of meanings arising from the same pre-text.

Projection and Simplification

In process drama, participants *literally* project themselves into the action. They become actors in the event, whose immediacy and spontaneity will prompt a necessarily simplified kind of response. At the same time, the necessity of building the dramatic world, responding to developments, and taking responsibility for maintaining this world in existence is likely to demand a level of objectivity and "unselfing" from the participants. The need to focus outward on these tasks may work to inhibit any kind of intense identification with a single character or role. This is the kind of "hallucinated participation" that Brecht distrusted in conventional theatre and that, in some types of roleplay, may edge the explorations toward a kind of complacent self-therapy. Brecht believed that the actor should not strive to become an incarnation of the character, but instead should aim to *expose* it. Heathcote echoed this when she pointed out that she achieves effective drama from students by taking their minds off of themselves. A further degree of objectivity in the participants will arise through the different kinds of observer-participant stances they adopt within the structure of the drama. There is both distance and presence. As Peter Brook puts it, distance is a commitment to total meaning and presence is a commitment to the living moment.[36] In *The Seal Wife,* the participants operated as writers, editors, and directors as well as actors within the drama. The work evoked a different level of engagement and a unique inner drama within each participant, just as in any successful theatre event.

In process drama, any development of characterization is a process of discovery, as it is in conventional theatre. The initial outline as well as the detail of the character has to be discovered through the encounter. As Bradbrook puts it, the unfocused aspects of character work within the minds of those who encounter them, like yeast in bread.[37] In process drama, elements of character will not be invented necessarily in advance but will consist of behavioral possibilities discovered in response to circumstance. Elements of character will be discerned as they surface in the immediacy of the dramatic encounter, and these discoveries will not be made necessarily only by the individuals undertaking particular roles. Instead, the possibilities of the roles that arise in the drama are likely to be explored, articulated, and developed by the entire group. Like both the structure and the plot, notions of character in process drama are necessarily retrospective, and only after the event is complete will it be possible to reflect fully on the characters that have emerged.

All discussions of character in theatre have been defined as discussions of value. The concept of character implies a sense of control, a system of moral and ethical values, and one which is created in personal choices. A significant aspect of process drama is that it makes it possible to *discover* these values within the dramatic action, instead of responding to values determined in advance. Rather than being a less elaborate and articulate version of "real" acting, engagement in process drama offers participants the opportunity to explore and realize a range of values and identities and experiment with alternate versions of humanity.

As people mature, they must discover their identity, define themselves, and invent themselves in the light of the possible roles that society has to offer them. The best way of discovering ourselves and learning our powers and potentialities is through our encounters with others, both real and imaginary. Through the dramatic roles and worlds that are available vicariously in theatre and directly in process drama, we can learn both who we are and what we may be. It is this that makes the essential nature of both theatre and process drama profoundly educational.

Expectations:
Time in Process Drama
and Theatre

■ **Time is an essential aesthetic element** in several of the arts, particularly in music, literature, and theatre. In theatre, time is a key structural principle in the development of the event. A central concern of all drama, even that which does not aim to present any kind of story, is the attempt to wrest precise moments of experience from the remorseless flux of time. While dramatic time apparently halts this flow, actual time continues to pass. This is also true of process drama where, within a certain timespan, it is possible to work within the tight causal structure of linear form or to operate in a more impressionistic, fragmented, panoramic, and open mode.

Temporal Elsewheres

In traditional dramatic organization, a fictional past is woven into the concerns of the dramatic present, while things to come are foreshadowed. There must be an immediate and surreptitious planting of an embryo future in a reported past for the dramatic world to take hold. Typically, the playwright establishes a sense of what has gone before, allows a significant accumulation of events, and creates an urgent sense of expectation so that the dramatic action develops significance for the audience. The past and the future meet in that perpetual present which is the most essential characteristic of time in the theatre.

As critics have pointed out repeatedly, a play is a sequence of "present moments," each of which moves away to become part of the past. The accumulated dramatic experience these moments afford must be sufficient to create tension and the anticipation of a possible resolution. Even in plays structured in a nonlinear way, an accretion of detail, image, and action will occur and recur and expectations will be raised. In plays structured in a circular manner, this resolution may be a recognition that there can be no resolution. The accumulation of present moments is, at the same time, preparation. Shadows of the past cannot stalk the future unless the dramatic experience includes this growth of significance, this cumulative effect. This accumulation may not always involve plot, but, as in Beckett's work, memory and desire resonate in a timeless present.

Unlike narrative, the direction of drama is not toward the present but aims at something beyond. The dominant dramatic mode deals with future commitments and consequences and exhibits a present filled with a sense of its own future. As spectators, we assist in the construction of the dramatic world by working to make a coherent pattern from the elements provided. We struggle to piece together all of the dramatic information we receive, to transform all of the stimuli projected by the dramatic event into a comprehensible sequence, and to anticipate outcomes. In conventional theatre events, the dramatist exploits this sense of anticipation and satisfies expectations by fulfilling them. The sense of destiny is paramount. In Langer's memorable phrase, persons in drama are "makers of the future."[1]

Where a traditional causal plot does not predominate, the event will still be patterned through a series of repetitions, variations, and combinations. Here, because psychological characterization is destabilized, transformational characters are defined by the shifting patterns of the dramatic interactions. Dramatic structure is severed from story and character and focuses on discourse, where past, present, and future may echo, overlap, and intermingle. This kind of non-causal organization is among the many possibilities available in process drama.

Double Time

For the audience in the theatre, time in the imagined world of the play operates in two ways. First, there is the experience of a "now" moving toward an as yet undiscovered future, but as the play proceeds there will also be a sense of time viewed retrospectively and already patterned. It is possible to identify these two aspects in terms of their "particular" and "universal" implications:

> The aesthetic life always contains two moments. During one of these, which can be called that of discovery, we accept the aesthetic object as a unique particular . . . During the other, which can be called that of assimilation, we make the aesthetic object

part of the body of experience and it assumes a universal reference because of the context and the direction that it gives to our
regard of other particulars.[2]

Although we may not usually think of a dramatic event as an aesthetic object, our response may be of this double nature. The experience of process drama readily encompasses both discovery and
assimilation. It is unlikely that the "present time" of an essentially
improvised event like process drama will seem any less arresting
than that of a scripted play. In fact, the knowledge that the work is
actually evolving for the first time should materially promote the
sense of a "now" moving toward what is, for the participants, a genuinely undisclosed future. It is this feature, above all, that gives improvised drama a sometimes overwhelming sense of risk, a powerful
vertiginous quality.

[In process drama, although the sense of time viewed retrospectively and already patterned may at first appear to be problematic for
participants, this need not present insuperable difficulties.] Dorothy
Heathcote, for example, typically uses a number of reflective approaches in order to produce a sense of patterned time, of universal
reference. Her concern to view time retrospectively goes hand in
hand with the kind of spontaneous encounter that is the hallmark of
her work and immediately distinguishes it from the kinds of improvised drama that remain brief, action-oriented, and unreflective.

In process drama the end is genuinely unforeseen by both leader
and participants. Where the work is conceived as following even a
loose, causal sequence, the task is to "plant" an embryo future, accumulate a number of increasingly significant events, and develop a
sense of time viewed retrospectively, without the participants necessarily being required to construct in advance elaborate biographies
for the roles they play or to build the plot in reverse. In *Frank Miller,*
the sense of the past was the driving impulse behind the drama, but
it was unnecessary to articulate this past in any detail. Because the
facts remained enigmatic and ambiguous, the sense of the past actually gained in power.

The Complexities of Dramatic Time

A plot is an organization that humanizes time by giving it form. A traditionally organized play may give time a shape, but what is important
is not calendar time but the fact that it is possible to engage in the contemplation of an action in which cause and effect have been made un-
usually clear. For this kind of contemplation to occur, it is essential that

some significant performance time must elapse. Since Aristotle, it has been clear that as far as the plot is concerned, a certain duration of the dramatic action is necessary, and this duration must be one that, while significant, may easily be encompassed by the memory.[3]

The kind of change that is a key element in theatre has to unfold over time. Through the demands of the action, the dramatic protagonists grow mentally, morally, or emotionally to the limits of their development. Shakespeare wrote of the "two-hour traffic" of the stage, and this may be approximately the timespan that must elapse if a form is to be fulfilled and if we are to be capable of making sense of the unfolding dramatic action. The time of the imagined world of the play must be enacted within the time in which actors and audience agree to be together, that is, in real time.

> "Time" and time, "world" and world, actors and audience, must intersect. This is the encounter which is theatre.[4]

Whether we are spectators at a play or participants in process drama, the duration of the event and its temporal dimension must give us the opportunity to

- apprehend the situation before us
- infer the past from which it has sprung
- grasp the relationships between acts and their consequences, or acts and their variations
- develop expectations and see these expectations fulfilled or denied

Where the dramatic structure is not tightly causal, the event will still require a temporal dimension that allows actions and events to be patterned in some fashion, perhaps cyclically or panoramically. Nonlinear patterns will need to be set up very clearly, so that a different kind of expectation is evoked from the audience. Beckett's *Krapp's Last Tape,* for example, begins with a highly patterned and repetitive sequence of movements without any verbal accompaniment. We begin to anticipate recurring variations and elaborations, rather than the unfolding of a conventional plot.

The One-Act Play

It is worth noting that although there are many great plays that last longer in performance than two hours, there are very few short plays of the first rank. Some of the ways that dramatists have employed time as an element when performance time is severely limited may help to determine whether a significant duration of actual time is essential in process drama. Naturalistic one-act plays by such playwrights as Synge, Lady Gregory, and Chekhov take a form that resembles that of the folktale or of a dramatized joke or anecdote. Many brief improvisations share a corresponding structure in performance. *The Farmer and the Hooker* improvisation from Second City falls into this category. Jokes, anecdotes, and mimicry are all tightly structured quasi-histrionic performances, containing dramatic exposition, tension, and reversal.

After a number of experiments, Eugene O'Neill came to regard the one-act play as an unsatisfactory form for his purposes, while recognizing it as "a fine vehicle for something poetical," for creating the kind of spiritual feeling that could not be sustained throughout a long play.[5] In less naturalistic short plays, such as Synge's *Riders to the Sea,* Wilder's *The Happy Journey,* and the verse plays of Yeats, time is deliberately exploited. Performance time must be limited, however, if these effects are to last.

It is certainly possible for even brief improvisations to be very intense. In the following example, Keith Johnstone describes an improvisation that possesses something of a poetical and time-transcending quality.

> Anthony Trent played being a prisoner in a cell. Lucy Fleming arrived, I don't remember how, and he endowed her with invisibility. At first he was terrified, but she calmed him down and said she had come to rescue him. She led him out of the prison and as he stepped free he fell dead.[6]

A similar kind of intensity is at work in Synge's *Riders to the Sea.* Time is almost unbearably contracted and foreshortened, so that we scarcely have time to dread Bartley's death by drowning before our anticipation is fulfilled by the sight of his dripping corpse. Every detail in the play foreshadows the approaching tragedy, from the clothes of Bartley's recently drowned brother to the "white boards" that will provide a decent coffin. Synge was fully aware of the limitations of the one-act form. He felt that the concentration demanded by a short play allows the dramatist to give only the headings and suggestions of what ought, if truthfully developed, to become full scenes.[7] Many brief improvisations, particularly those designed for performance, are necessarily limited to "headings and suggestions." Process drama, by definition, is not restricted to a single episode, but it need not necessarily be lengthy to achieve its effects.

The Fragmentation of Experience

Many dramatists reject the hypnotic power of the neat linear form and choose to represent the incompleteness and discontinuity of life in images, patterns, and fragments of experience. Similarly, in science the concept of "field" has replaced the idea of time unfolding in a linear way. Like artists in other media, playwrights have attempted to escape from the tyranny of time's progression in drama and instead capture the complex dimensions of a present burdened with layers of memory.

At the start of *That Time,* by Beckett, the Listener's face alone is visible, while three voices (his own) come at him from both sides and above. The entire play is a pattern of repetitions. Voices and memories come from outside time and yet are located in the real time of the play's brief performance. The form of this kind of drama is especially elusive, because its subject matter is the flux of time itself.

Beckett, only one of many modern playwrights who have taken time itself as a theme, shows his obsession in the very titles of his plays—*Waiting for Godot, Endgame, Krapp's Last Tape, Happy Days,* as well as *That Time.* He has overcome the difficulties of employing time as a dramatic element in a brief compass by turning time itself into a central thematic and controlling feature. The very intensity that results demands a brevity of form. Thornton Wilder experimented with condensing time and thereby making it his subject in his one-act play, *The Long Christmas Dinner,* where the rise and decline of a family over ninety years is contained in what appears to be a single Christmas. The static, unchanging quality of the occasion is counterpointed by the transformations in the family, so that the play becomes, in Szondi's phrase, "a secular mystery play about time."[8] Like other modern dramatists, Tennessee Williams regards time as so essential for the dramatist that the influence of "life's destroyer, time" must be somehow worked into the context of the play. It is, he suggests, the "arrest of time" that will give plays their depth and significance.[9]

Attempts to explore dramatic discontinuity can be seen as contextual rather than linear. To absorb an audience in tensions of *context* rather than *sequence,* both verbal and visual imagery must function together. The implications for the playwright of this way of working are considerable, particularly in terms of characterization. An example of a modern contextual character in a mainstream drama is in Miller's *Death of a Salesman,* where the operation of time is interior. Character development is vertical rather than horizontal. In many respects, it may be easier for participants in process drama to generate and evolve "vertical" characterizations of this kind, rather than to attempt the development of characters and plots that unfold in a linear way. The implications of these attempts will include changes of perspective, especially in character development, and an increased emphasis on visual elements.

Gertrude Stein, whose experiments influenced the American avant-garde and in particular the work of Richard Foreman, attempted to avoid what she called the "syncopated time" of conventional drama, in which the spectators' response is always a beat behind what is happening on stage. Her solution was to attempt to structure plays without any narrative progression whatsoever. These static compositions, where the play is perceived as a landscape—a panorama of present moments—are experienced almost as a private meditative dream through a series of nonsequential stage pictures.[10]

Circular Time

The type of theatre event that relies on the creation of powerful images, intense moods, or dream-like states is likely to be most effective when it is presented in brief episodes. The optimal length of absurd or symbolist drama, like that of poetic drama, will probably correspond to that of the one-act play. Many modern plays of this kind make their impact by using time in a circular or "bracketed" fashion. Circular time can be defined as a series of events contained in a single unit that repeats itself without a causal chain linking the sequence, as in Ionesco's *The Lesson.* The apparently random quality of this kind of drama appears to be shared by Happenings, although, in fact, such events are usually constructed carefully in order to produce striking and memorable juxtapositions of temporal and other elements. What is missing in the kind of drama that relies on circular time is what Langer calls the "ominous forward movement of consequential action."[11] The one-act play *Aria da Capo,* by Edna St. Vincent Millay, is a neat example of a less random circular form, where the violent action of the play changes nothing and is bracketed by the same opening and closing dialogue.

A short piece by Theatre Machine, performed at the Royal Court Theatre in 1970, demonstrated that it is possible to exploit this kind of circularity to give shape to improvisation. In this improvisation, four priests bustle reverentially about an altar, on which stands an agonizingly crucified figure, a fifth actor. There is a strict hierarchy among the priests, and they continually give orders to each other. The priest with the lowest status becomes more and more oppressed by the others. The Christ-figure grows bored with these ministrations and begins surreptitiously to make faces at the priests and make increasingly rude gestures. As he becomes more and more outrageous, the priests eventually became aware of his behavior. He is ordered down from the altar, and the least important priest is promoted to his place. The reverential ritual begins once more, and the formerly idealized Christ-figure is now the most oppressed of all. There is a symmetry to this reversal of roles. The circular shape of this painfully funny piece is powerful and satisfying, as are the ritual and game elements that provide much of its inner structure.[12]

Absolute circularity seems to deny the dominant dramatic principle of cause and effect, and circularity is more often relative than absolute. Some degree of change and progression is usually observable. A significant example of the operation of bracketed time is *Waiting for Godot*. Here, actions occur within the "dawn-dusk" bracket, but are not causally related to each other and are not repeated exactly or in the same order. Vladimir and Estragon have no grip on time. Their "present moment" indicates a complete discontinuity and is disturbing to both the characters and the audience precisely because of the absence of any true relationship to past and future. They have no sense of their lives that will give meaning to the present in which they are trapped, nor can they look forward to any sure release. All they know of time is that it passes. Time has lost its meaning but paradoxically has acquired a total significance. Beckett is squandering time, putting the play outside all temporal reality while apparently immersed in its categories.

> The failure of memory in Beckett is . . . a built-in convenience by
> which the play is able to escape all moorings in time and space
> that might lock the characters into a causal history.[13]

It is not surprising that, according to Esslin, the play was instantly understood by the convicts at San Quentin, who were "doing time" in the same sense as Didi and Gogo.[14] Their time is most precisely measured, but its significance is only that it passes. The critic who said on leaving the first performance of *Godot* that it was like being let out of prison had gotten the play exactly right. There is "nothing to be done," because time would have passed anyway.

Pattern and Rhythm

In his famous formulation, Aristotle, as well as insisting that a dramatic action must be of a certain length, expected that it would contain a beginning, a middle, and an end. In other words, within a sufficient timespan the drama is initiated, articulated, and fulfilled or consummated. Traditionally, each dramatic situation arises out of what has preceded it and leads to the anticipation of further change until the end of expectation is reached. The dramatist shapes these situations into an appropriate pattern of events, a task that those working in process drama must achieve in the unfolding and ephemeral moment as they call the dramatic world into being. This sense of pattern is necessary to give the dramatic world authenticity and structure. The development of a sense of pattern for audience or participants usually requires a significant span of performance time, although other noncausal patterns may be achieved in the compass of a short play, as in the earlier examples of circularity. This kind of patterning allows the piece to circumvent the dominance of cause and effect. A rhythm of action arises when dramatic situations are so connected and continuous that one indirectly or directly motivates the next.

There is also another kind of rhythm at work—the rhythm of involvement and disengagement that occurs in human attention. This rhythm can provide the basis for segmenting theatre into units of time, and these units will be the contextual frames within which the drama evolves. Each unit will have a rhythmic character in terms of the degree of its intensity. These rhythmic segments of action provide the basic building blocks of drama. The dynamic quality of this variation in intensity is at the heart of the dramatic effect, and this can occur even when the organization of the play is nontraditional. As Dewey puts it,

> The connection of intensity and extensity and of both with tension is not a verbal matter. There is no rhythm save where there is alternation of compression and release. Resistance . . . accumulates tension that renders energy intense.[15]

The rhythmic qualities of a piece of theatre are closely involved with the development of dramatic tension in the work. Without tension, there can be no articulation or fulfillment. The dramatic event, whether organized traditionally or after some more elusive pattern, is filled with physical, emotional, and intellectual tensions, all of which give quality to the passage of time.

At another level, in both theatre and process drama, there is a rhythmic quality in the alteration of the participants' and spectators' engagement. This may spiral from intense involvement through disengagement, detachment, and distance back to increased involvement.

Repetition

The question of the repeatability of the theatre event was discussed in an earlier chapter. Another important type of repetition is that which develops in the course of the work, is part of the pattern of the piece, and is almost synonymous with rhythm. A work of art in which no element was ever repeated would be impossible to apprehend. Repetition in any art form gives unity and integrity to the work and organizes our perceptions. It is essentially rhythmic and operates through ordered variation. Its presence implies variation, alternation, and above all, contrast, and therefore the existence of other elements. Repetition and variation, or "re-incorporation," as Johnstone calls it, will give a satisfying shape and balance to improvisation and process drama.[16] Unless the work occurs over a sufficient timespan, however, it will be impossible to observe these qualities in operation.

Some of the most obvious of the repetitions and contrasts that are at the heart of traditional theatre are those of relationships, ideas, and images. *King Lear,* for example, contains many different aspects of the relationships between fathers and children. Other repeated and contrasted themes are madness and disguise. The Fool's injunction to the King, "See better, Lear!" allows us to parallel Lear's metaphorical blindness with the appalling blinding of Gloucester. Each recurrence or variation is new, but at the same time, an extension and reminder of what has gone before.

Repetition and variation are employed by other art forms that possess temporal structures. These patterns are among the foremost aids to the organization of artistic materials. In the dominant dramatic mode, as distinct from the avant-garde work discussed earlier, the repetitions of images or themes in theatre depend on a logical and developing structure of meaning. But the dramatic character, unlike, for example, the musical theme, can never step twice into the same river. All of the elements of the drama that exist continuously through time, and their repetition and variation, are essential in the task of creating structure and providing continuity. The principle of repetition and variation is at the heart of the work of Beckett and Pinter.

Continuity

Continuity—particularly continuity of scenes—is a prime concern in dramatic structure. By grouping elements into units and weaving a thread of similarity through continually changing events, continuity mitigates complexity and ensures a sense of unity and coherence. Even in a brief piece of improvisation that does not encompass a number of scenes, we might expect elements to persist and to be echoed or repeated, so that they can begin to provide an internal structure for our experience of the event. In *The Farmer and the Hooker,* for example, both characters have children (repetition) and carry photos and tattoos of these children (variation). Where such resonances occur, they are profoundly satisfying.

Continuing elements, for example, the actor/character or particular settings, places, relationships, verbal and nonverbal images, and actions, connect or contrast units of time within a dramatic event and establish its structure—the thread weaving through the work. As well as the element actually present, there are also degrees of psychological continuity or presence in characters who are hidden, expected, or talked about and who therefore provide the possibility of continuity. The complex variations of time and place, and the ways in which characters are discussed and described in their absence—for example, Shakespeare's Antony and Cleopatra, at one end of the scale, and Beckett's Godot and Synge's Bartley at the other—demonstrate this mental continuity and build the world of the play. Egypt and Cleopatra come into focus as they are discussed in Rome, and we grasp the significance of Rome and Caesar in their impact on Egypt and Cleopatra. We try to make sense of Godot's possible arrival or begin to dread the death of Bartley and its effect on the three women whose fear we have shared.

The provocation and channeling of our expectations about these characters and events is essentially *structural* and will operate equally effectively in improvised drama. As the participants anxiously anticipate the arrival of Frank Miller, they begin to create details of his character and background. In *The Farmer and the Hooker* improvisation, the actors tease the spectators and first arouse their expectations before reversing them.

Time in Process Drama

> In improvisation there is only one time . . . Memory and intention (which postulate past and future) and intuition (which indicates

an eternal present) are fused . . . Improvisation is also called ex-
temporization, meaning both "outside of time" and "from time".[17]

What is true of improvisation is also true of process drama and is
more readily achieved. Dramatic worlds are never simple and static,
but are a complex sequence of circumstances. Although process
drama can create a fictional "now" with great economy and immediacy,
it is the power of a succession of dramatic "presents" where both past
and future meet that is so rarely created or exploited in other kinds of
improvised drama. The very spontaneity and ephemerality of the action seems to militate against an understanding and use of dramatic
time by the participants. Dramatic worlds that arise from improvisation are typically very brief, and however skillfully they may develop,
there is little actual performance time in which they can work their effects. Burns has noted this neglect of time as a structural element in
improvisation and believes it results from the conventions on which
this apparently unconventional theatre form is established.

> The new theatre of improvisation and semi-improvisation rests
> not so much on timelessness as on the convention that action is
> being created instant by instant, and hence that traditional dra-
> matic conventions of time can be disregarded. This means that
> the actors must be sensitive to "timing" but not necessarily to any
> structural concept of the time within which the action takes place.
> An improvisation is ideally open-ended. It should be able to start
> and end at any moment, when the actors feel that they have ac-
> complished something or run out of ideas.[18]

These notions of the operation of time in improvisation are limited,
but may correspond to many people's experience as spectators of the
form. Burns's use of the word *convention* seems to suggest that even
the apparent spontaneity of the activity is an illusion.

Famous People

The following example demonstrates some of the ways in which the
temporal dimension may be manipulated in process drama. In this
work with highschool students, the teacher launches the dramatic
world with two questions. These questions arise from the setting and
allow the participants to develop their individual roles very gradually.

The teacher explains the role expectations. Everyone in the group is very
famous in a particular field and has reached the top of his profession.

They are famous because of what they have achieved themselves, not because of their family or partner. They are not a "real" person, like a present-day celebrity. If they can't decide immediately their field of excellence, it will still be possible to join in the activity.

Episodes	Drama Elements
In role as a talk show host presenter, the teacher welcomes them to the studio to discuss the advantages and disadvantages of being famous. The host asks each person in turn to say, in a single sentence, the best thing about being famous. The answers are predictable—fame, money, respect, freedom, material possessions. Some begin to define the area for which they are famous—"speaking as a scientist . . ." or "In the music business . . ." When everyone has spoken, she asks a further question: "What, for each of you, is the worst thing about being famous?"	The encounter, a TV talk show, follows a familiar format that regulates and controls the interaction. A further control is provided by the two guiding **questions**. The teacher's role here is essentially as a support to the roles being developed by the participants. She repeats, reflects on, and elaborates the initially sketchy responses. This second question deepens the responses. Now, fame is seen as a burden, and the celebrities as confined, threatened, and afraid to fail.
In small groups, the students create tableaux. These are family photos that show the celebrity as a child. Something in the image should suggest an aspect, skill, or quality of the person that could retrospectively suggest the field in which they achieved preeminence. A "photo" is prepared for each person in the group.	There is an interesting time shift here for the students. The first activity required them to project into the **future**; now they must create the **past**. These images are interrogated for the aspects of character they reveal.

Having begun to define the imagined world, not through a situation, but through the roles with which the students have been endowed, the teacher narrates the next section. Some crisis—mental, physical, emotional—has caused the famous people to feel unable to carry on. This crisis should be something that they would not share easily with anyone else, but that the media would like to know. They have decided to return home, although they have not been back for a number of years. Thus the drama begins at a moment of change, when the famous person has reached the height of fame and fortune but is about to face the disintegration of this success. At this point, the students are asked to work in pairs, with one person temporarily relinquishing the role of the celebrity.

In pairs, A is the famous person and B is a close associate—an agent, manager, or personal secretary. A "telephones" B in order to cancel arrangements for an upcoming tour, appearance, speech, game, or performance, without giving a clear explanation. B tries to persuade A to honor the arrangements already made.

This conversation is carried on with the students sitting back to back or side by side so that there is no eye contact. The reason for the cancellation should remain ambiguous. There is a **game** element to this conversation as the celebrity tries to conceal the real reason for leaving.

The teacher discusses with the B people the famous people's states of mind. Fears, suspicions, and anxieties are shared.

The famous people are **audience** to this exchange and begin to develop a sense of their own states of mind as well as of their significance to others.

At this point, the first session of the drama ends. In order to pick up some of the feeling quality that had been developing, the teacher chooses to play a game called "Pruie."

In this game, one person is secretly chosen to be the "Pruie." This person remains silent at all times. The rest close their eyes, and their task is to find the Pruie. This they achieve by saying "Pruie?" to everyone they touch. If there is no response, they have found the Pruie and then hold on and become silent themselves. Eventually, after much searching, everyone is linked to the Pruie.

The **game** is an experience of exclusion and inclusion and can carry a degree of **tension** for the participants. It is set outside the time of the dramatic action.

Now the task is to establish the atmosphere of the hometown to which the famous people are returning. With their eyes shut, each contributes a detail of some sight, sound, or reminiscence of the place.

This composite "scene painting" creates the sense of a typical small community, where very little changes with the years.

The participants are asked at this point if they want to remain as famous people or if they want to become townspeople. Half of the group decides to remain in role as the celebrities; the rest become school friends, neighbors, or acquaintances who knew the celebrities before they became famous.

The students work in pairs, with one as the celebrity and the other as friend or acquaintance. They meet accidentally in a location in which they can talk without interruption. The celebrity carries the burden of the "crisis," which he or she may not feel comfortable about sharing.

This meeting is quite an intense encounter. In it, the celebrities recreate their **past lives**, and the **memories** they share with their friends. Some of these may be painful. Some couples may find it difficult to establish common ground with their townsperson.

The townspeople come together with the teacher to discuss the famous people they have just encountered. Many feel almost sorry for the celebrity to whom they have talked; others resent the fame and fortune they have themselves missed. In some cases, the celebrity has confided their troubles to their old friend.

This is a reflective activity. The celebrities are again **audience** to this interchange and get a view of themselves as lonely, needy, patronizing, and arrogant.

Next, the teacher talks to the famous people about their visit home. Has it given them the sense of peace they were seeking? How does the place appear to them now? Many are disillusioned and cynical, although a few have seen an image of what they might have been had they stayed at home.

This time, the townspeople are **audience** and hear what the famous people really think about them and their home. In many cases the remarks are dismissive, if not downright hostile.

That night, the townspeople remember an incident when they were young, in which they helped, saved, or outshone the famous person. Working in groups, the students recreate some of these scenes.

The other groups are **audience** to the performances of these scenes. The townspeople have an opportunity to reflect on their unrealized dreams and ambitions. The **past** is being brought to life.

The teacher meets the townspeople in role as an editor for a series of publications and TV programs specializing in scandal and the lives of the rich and famous. She has heard that they have met some celebrities

In effect, the editor is asking them to betray their former friends. Some are horrified by the exploitative possibilities that are being proposed; others are eager to put the public right about the real na-

and offers to pay them for any inside stories they may have on their famous friends.

ture of the famous person. No decision is required at this point.

The famous people meet their old friends one more time. Some reveal that they've been approached by the editor; others do not. The famous people tell their friends their plans for the future. Some decide to remain; others plan to return to their former lives.

This interaction is naturally affected by the previous episode, but it will be important that the social niceties are maintained. There is **roleplaying within the role.**

Working in groups, the students create a newspaper headline and story or TV item that reveals whether or not the celebrity has been betrayed, given up their career and returned to their home town, or continued with their current success.

A variety of endings for each of the famous people are determined by the students. This episode also projects into the **future.**

The final episode is in pairs. Here, the celebrities imagine that they are at the end of their careers and are being interviewed by a young journalist who is writing a feature about them. They recall the particular moment in their lives when they were in crisis and returned home, and then fill in some of the details since then.

This reflective activity, although it has moved far into the **future,** is focused firmly on the **past,** the time they have just lived through. The famous people are required to build a life in retrospect, as they did earlier in the sequence, and to reflect on their triumphs and failures.

In this process drama, both past and future intermingle. The story does not move in a linear way, but through a series of increasingly intense encounters. There is a constant tension between what the famous people have been and what they may be in the future.

If process drama is to achieve significant dramatic form and complexity of meaning it is essential for the participants in the event to become sensitive to time as a *structural* concept and to understand and be able to employ the dramatic conventions of time as principal ordering features in the work. The recognition that the drama can be developed through units of action or episodes will put the complexities of dramatic time at the service of the participants. Even the briefest improvisation is likely to suggest a context of past actions and intentions and to imply future consequences. Working in scenic form, with a sense of the possibilities offered by dramatic time, the leader will be able to explore and articulate these implications. Units or episodes may be selected so as to exploit a dimension of time and emphasize either the past, present, or future. The segmentation of the work into episodes need not necessarily be abrupt or arbitrary. It will be guided by the rhythm of involvement and disengagement, by the pull of tensions within the work. An intense moment of debate or confrontation may be followed by a reflective phase oriented toward the past, or by a planning phase where future possibilities are investigated. In reaching back into the past or forward into the future, the protagonists may repeat, modify, or reestablish relationships.

This kind of scenic organization prolongs actual performance time, releases the participants from the pressure of remaining in an extended improvised encounter, and allows pattern, rhythm, and continuity to become significant in the work. The evolution of process drama in relation to time as a structural principle will allow the participants to rest in the past, while forging the present and foreshadowing the future. However ephemeral, and whether traditional or avant-garde, every kind of theatre event, including process drama, overcomes time by its capacity for infinite transformations.

Conspiracies:
Audience and Participation

■ **All forms of theatre,** including improvised drama, have in common the need for an audience. Any act of conscious self-presentation implies an other or others to whom the presentation is being offered, and the human presence that is at the heart of theatre always includes the presence of the audience. The spectators and their participation in the encounter define it as theatre, which does not mean merely what the actors do in the presence of the audience. It also refers to the encounter between them. The spectators are essential for the realization of the work, and without them no theatre event is complete.

> It is an indisputable fact that a dramatic work, whatever it may be, is designed to be listened to by a number of persons united and forming an audience, that this is its very essence, that this is a necessary condition of its existence . . . This then we can insist on: No audience, no play. The audience is the necessary and inevitable condition to which dramatic art must accommodate its means.[1]

In experimental and improvised theatre, this central preoccupation with audience focuses on the relationship between the viewer and the viewed. This concern, however, is by no means limited to avant-garde theatre, although it is there that efforts to transform the alignment of performers and audience may be most noticeable. Pavis insists that since the time of Aristotle, the emotional reaction of the spectator in the theatre has been the aesthetic and ideological touchstone of the art.[2]

The essential literal truth of the theatrical situation seems simple enough. A group of people is being watched and listened to by another, usually larger, group of people. The first group, the actors, pretend to be fictional characters in invented places and situations. They

create a fiction, a pretense, and those who watch accept and participate in that pretense. The entire occurrence is a kind of conspiracy
by both the watchers and the watched to establish and believe in the
imaginary world that is being created and presented. Although it appears that the actors are in control of this conspiracy, the audience
can be regarded as the senior partner in this relationship, calling the
tune, as it were, and even indirectly employing all those engaged in
creating the theatrical experience. In this view, the dominant figure
in the theatre is not the playmaker but the playgoer, who can be persuaded but never commanded to participate in the event. The spectators initiate the theatrical communicative process. Their apparent
passivity in the interaction is an active choice.

The spectator has been increasingly installed at the core of the
event in such disparate disciplines as science and literary criticism.
This refocusing has also taken place in theatre studies where
semiologists have revealed the extent to which the spectator's role in
theatre is the reverse of passive. To some extent, the actors and director are also spectators to the work, as well as being active in its composition, but they are not the masters of its meaning. The experience of
theatre demands an active mediation by the spectators, who speculate,
make assumptions, apply interpretations, and develop expectations
about the make-believe world that is unfolding before them. They labor to produce meaning from the dramatic representation which is, by
its nature, discontinuous and fragmentary. The successful theatre
event will be sufficiently defined to give impetus and direction to these
efforts, but open enough to evoke speculation and complex projections. But at the same time that the spectators struggle to "read" and
make sense of what they see, they are fully aware of its illusory nature.
As Pavis puts it, the theatre event always says in the same breath, "I
am a fiction"and "You must believe in me."[3]

For the playmakers, the audience is there and not there, ignored
yet necessary. While recognizing the necessity of each others' existence, on another level the spectators acquiesce in seeing primarily
the characters in the play rather than the actors playing those parts,
and the actors generally behave as if the spectators were invisible.
For the actor, the spectator is a partner who is rarely acknowledged
and yet must not be forgotten in all decisions that are taken about the
presentation of the event. Every change in the alignment of actors
and audience, even altering the physical location of the spectators in
relation to the performers, will bring about a difference in response.
As Barthes puts it,

> The Theatre is precisely that practice which calculates the place
> of things as they are observed: if I set the spectacle here, the
> spectator will see this; if I put it elsewhere, he will not.[4]

The spectators' point of view, literally, determines their perception of events and their attitudes when confronted by the actors.

Some forms of theatre will, of their nature, demand a greater degree of separation than others. Both the struggle for authenticity at the naturalistic end of the spectrum and the presentation of stage magic at the other will demand considerable actual separation of actors from audience. The illusion of naturalism is not laden with obvious formal conventions, but the audience must be sufficiently distanced both physically and psychologically from the action for the illusion to remain unchallenged. At the completion of the event, the applause does not merely demonstrate approval and reward, but precisely indicates the limits of illusion.

The degree of isolation of the spectators from the action may vary from one period of theatre history to another, but is always more or less sharply marked. It appears that unless the spectators are set apart from the action on stage they cannot contemplate it, and this separation must not be merely physical but also psychological. Paradoxically, the deepest response to the work seems to be made possible by distance, disengagement, and detachment.

Privacy and Distance

The anonymity and privacy of the spectator in the theatre is, according to Wilshire, an "inviolable rule," regulating the intercourse of actor and audience, world and "world." Because they are isolated from the action on the stage, often protected by the darkness and separated by a physical barrier from the actors, the spectators are free to speculate, interpret, and determine the meaning of what they see. They are also free to feel, protected both by the physical and the aesthetic distance between them and the world of the play. As individuals, the spectators determine the intellectual and emotional depth to which they permit the performance to penetrate their consciousness. It is because of this protection and distance that they are free to respond.

An important part of any aesthetic experience is the knowledge that it is just that, and that the parentheses of form are safely in place. The bracketing and distancing of the aesthetic point of view allows the spectator access to different degrees of detachment and involve-

ment. The history of the theatre can be viewed as a history of flirta-
tion with the psychical distance between stage and audience, and for
Bullough, both staging and dramaturgy are closely bound up with
the evolution of distance.[5] Distance is a factor in all art, and any theatrical performance runs a special risk of loss of distance. The actual,
physical presence of the actors as vehicles of dramatic art presents
difficulties that no other art has to face in quite the same way, and the
fact that we are drawn intensely into the drama makes the preserva-
tion of distance more, rather than less, important. The ideal audience
is one that maintains some sense of detachment. The spectators encounter a world in which they cannot interfere, but over which they
exercise the control of knowledge, and which they observe with a
balance of sympathy and detachment. They enjoy the double pleasure of seeing through another's consciousness while observing the
character, pleasures that include both identification and distance.

It is precisely because the real and imagined worlds are separated that they can illuminate each other in these ways. The very in-
dependence and autonomy of the world of the theatre provides the
foundation for its capacity to offer an independent way of knowing.
But this supposedly autonomous domain exists by embracing an audience from another world.

> The mutual contamination of the world of the theatre and the
> world of the audience is not just unavoidable, it is fundamental to
> the theatre's structure and function.[6]

This "contamination" has been the subject of active exploration by
many avant-garde ensembles, and particularly by those using improvisation as the basis of their work.

Audience Participation

Many critics suggest that the abolition of the distance between spectators and performers by any kind of audience participation is destructive not just of that distance but also of the drama itself. Under
the pressure of attempts at audience participation, what may result is
that the theatre splits apart into a physical life without imaginative
dimension and an imaginative life incapable of presence.[7]

"Frame breaking" of this kind is sometimes thought to make art
more lifelike but, paradoxically, breaking the frame by an invitation
to join in can destroy the integrity of the make-believe world and the
equilibrium of engagement and detachment between actors and audi-

ence. To attempt to come too close to the theatrical event may be to abolish it. The customary contract in theatre is that the audience has neither the right nor the obligation to participate directly in the dramatic action that is occurring on stage, but as we have seen, avant-garde ensembles frequently attempt to redraw this contract. In the kind of theatre that demands participation and tries to break the circle of illusion by drawing the audience into the action, the fundamental nature of the aesthetic experience will be altered.

In Happenings and in improvised theatre, the brackets that contain the unreal world are spaced more widely apart. It is easier to regard an object or a setting as fictitious than it is to feel an emotion as imaginary, and even, or perhaps especially, in participatory theatre, emotions will be felt. In these cases, the secure vulnerability of the audience will no longer be safeguarded by privacy and distance.

FRAMING THE AUDIENCE

Grotowski, in his experiments with the actor-audience relationship, struggled to find a thematic function, a role for his audiences within the dramatic world. He attempted to integrate them structurally into the play, not just by changes in the physical environment, but by imposing on them a psychological orientation so that they became "framed" within the world of the drama. These frames gave them a heightened consciousness of their function as particular kinds of spectators. In *Dr. Faustus* the spectators became guests at his "last supper," and in *The Constant Prince* they were framed as both voyeurs and witnesses.

Grotowski's experiments finally persuaded him of the artificiality of this kind of actor-audience relationship, and he came to recognize that physically mingling actors and spectators in an attempt at audience participation could create psychological barriers. Distancing the actors and the spectators in space allowed them to regain a psychic propinquity.

Attempts of this kind to erase the barriers between actors and audience are likely to define their separation even more sharply. The spectators become acutely aware, not only of the performers but of themselves, sensing that they have been cast in the role of a particular *kind* of audience, with a particular task to perform. They have become "theatricalized." Their isolation is not eliminated, but merely recharacterized. There is also an effect on the actors, whose function has changed. When they are made responsible for drawing the audience into the event, casting them in their roles, and modeling appropriate responses, there are implications for the actors' performance.

If their task is to stimulate an unrehearsed response from other actors or spectators as participants, they cannot take refuge in naturalism. To preserve the dramatic illusion in naturalistic theatre, the spectator must remain a voyeur of the imagined world. The paradox of naturalism is that it affirms both our intimacy with the dramatic world and our distance from it.

The notion of an area for negotiation between actors and spectators is based, for some critics, on an inability to distinguish between what is theatre and what is not. They insist that although "participationists" have supposed a fascinating middle ground, there is only a sharp frontier. For Pavis, the spectator and the actor operate on different planes. Exchanges between them can occur only in extreme cases where the actor does not play a role but *is* himself—in other words, where the dramatic world is sufficiently loosely bracketed to include the spectators. Pavis' example is the work of the Living Theatre, and it is worth noting that much of the work of this group was an attempt to achieve an "authenticity" of performance, where the actor could indeed "be himself."[8]

Although many innovative performance ensembles are interested in bringing the audience into a dynamic association with the action, where participation is directly invited by the performers only a limited range of responses may be allowed. The Living Theatre, which appeared on the surface to be unpredictable and open-ended, in reality restricted the actor-audience exchanges. The outcomes of these exchanges were anticipated by the company and were to some degree preprogrammed. When unexpected responses occurred, the actors found themselves unable to cope. It is clear that participation becomes more than an "illusionistic device" only when it can influence the tone or change the outcome of the performance. Where this potential for change was built into the play's structure, as in Schechner's *Dionysus in '69,* audience participation was found to disrupt the rhythm of the action and to reduce both the dramatic effectiveness of the structure and the ritual quality of the performance. Taken to its extreme, it made control of the performance impossible. Like the playwright or director in conventional theatre, the actors in participatory theatre are faced with the problem of immediately reorienting and controlling audience participation in the whole theatrical event. They must teach the audience the rules of the new game while that game is in progress. Where the audience retains conventional expectations of its own function in the event, this becomes an almost impossible task. In process drama, where the audience is framed inside the event, these rules are more easily negotiated and generated.

As Schechner's actors discovered when the spectators responded unexpectedly, it is not always possible to control audience involvement once it has been invited. Simon Callow describes an occasion when the Joint Stock theatre company performed *Devil's Island,* by David Hare, at Dublin's Abbey Theatre, as part of the annual Theatre Festival. The audience was seated on the stage and very soon began to heckle and interrupt the actors. The audience became so noisy and aggressive that eventually the performance was suspended. The actors were asked to return to the stage and explain their decision.

> The audience, now sitting in the stalls, were certainly in a combative mood . . . Clearly, the stage was regarded as a gladiatorial arena . . . Their underlying assumption about the relationship of the audience to the actors seemed to be that a state of suspended hostility was the norm, and that by varying the rules and inviting participation we must expect aggression. They were particularly adamant that you couldn't only vary *some* of the rules: one couldn't say "Participate in some scenes but not in others". . . Dublin clearly regarded theatre as a form of unarmed combat, in which only the fittest survived.[9]

Here, the combative spectators are clearly in the right, as Callow seems to accept. The actors wished to change the rules, but only for their own advantage. They had failed to grant the audience equal rights with the performers.

In spite of the interest that avant-garde dramatists, directors, and ensembles have shown in exploring the actor-audience relationship, and in particular the roles in which they cast their audiences, they may be mistaken in their understanding of the audience's role. An audience that is reviled is unjustly treated. It is the actors who are presumptuous in exceeding the privilege of their position. As the dramatist Arnold Wesker has put it, you don't jeer at people you've paralyzed because they can't walk.[10]

New Contracts

Even when there is no direct participation in the dramatic action, spectators at improvised theatre events tend to be drawn into a new kind of contract with the performers. The dramatic illusion is not canceled, but the spectators' illusionary nearness to the action is renegotiated. The conspiracy into which they enter acknowledges the fragility of the improvised dramatic world and heightens their sense of community, co-creation, and cooperation. When they recognize and employ the "rules of the game," as well as accept their responsibility in creating the event, the result can be an experience of considerable intensity. When the conspiracy fails, the event is likely to split apart, destroying the imagined world and any balance within the spectator between detachment and involvement. In spite of claims that the audience in an improvised event is more than usually "active" and not only "reads" the performance but also "writes" it, too, a gulf is likely to remain between performers and spectators. The former will be operating their own agenda, their own text, and inhabiting their own dramatic world, and although the spectators may be implicated in the creation of the event, it is almost impossible for them, while they remain characterized as a passive audience, to become genuine partners in co-creating the event and true transformers of the dramatic action. For this to happen, a new contract must be negotiated between performers and spectators, one indicating different powers and responsibilities.

Audience in Process Drama

The absence of an audience is one of the most obvious and distinguishing features of process drama. The imagined world is created by and for the participants themselves. In spite of the essential need for an audience to complete the theatre event, the lack of a separate audience in this kind of drama does not invalidate it as a theatre form. It is the participants in process drama who provide this sense of audience and complete the theatrical equation. The essentially implicit nature of the audience is accepted by Bolton, who sees the performance mode that implies an audience as being implicitly present in every improvised drama. Participants are in a continual state of tension between representing an experience and being *in* an experience. Expression and representation are not separate, but one contains the other, and there is a subtle movement between the two modes.[11] Process drama, like theatre, inevitably evokes a shared public meaning among the participants and like dramatic play, is invariably a display, a performance, even if the only spectators are the other participants.

The participants in process drama are faced with much the same task as the spectators in a theatre. They must also labor to make meaning as the parameters of the imaginary world are created and revealed. These details emerge gradually, are subject to change, and are not fully known until the work is ended. Even more obviously than a play in the theatre, the improvised world defines itself as it proceeds, rather than being set up in advance. The participants in process drama and the spectators in theatre are "negotiating meaning," but the former are not merely construing but also actively creating the imagined world.[12] The audience in a theatre waits for something to happen, but the participants in process drama *make* this "something" happen. Like spectators in the theatre, they live within two overlapping circles of experience—that of the dramatic world and that of their own actuality. But participants in process drama *actively* inhabit both the real world and the imagined world.

Spect-actors

The nature of this double existence is both exploited and clarified in the work of Augusto Boal. Although Boal is a director and a playwright who works largely through improvisation, his purpose is almost always didactic. The manifest aim of his work is to change people, to turn passive spectators into actors (in his word, "spect-actors") who will leave the privacy of the audience, enter the dramatic world, and transform the dramatic action.[13] In Boal's work, the two realms of stage and audience remain sharply differentiated, and only a handful of spectators are licensed to cross from one realm to the other. The audience does not cease to exist because some of its members have entered the actors' carefully defined theatrical "double space," where one can be both oneself and someone other than oneself. This transformation of spectator into performer is radically different from the kind of participation encouraged by many avant-garde ensembles.

According to Boal, when the spectators accept his challenge and actually penetrate the fictional world by taking over as participants-playwrights, they are able to make the dramatic crisis and its possible solutions come alive because they have come to belong actively in both the real and the fictional worlds. This is what he calls "the metaxis phenomenon," the total and simultaneous adherence to two different and autonomous worlds.[14] When the spectators become spect-actors, the heart of the event has moved from the stage to the auditorium. A new contract has been negotiated between spectators and performers.

Like Brecht, Boal believes that empathy and catharsis in the theatre are negative forces because they immobilize the audience. Brecht appealed to audiences to work for themselves, to remain detached and critical, and to resist seduction by the actor's craft or theatrical illusion. The purpose of his "alienation effect" is a call to become conscious of oneself as a spectator, to observe, to judge. It anticipates or freezes the action, interrupts the argument, and questions facile assumptions. It defamiliarizes perception and impedes any kind of "hallucinated" response. Boal works for greater actual involvement of his audience, but also, paradoxically, increased detachment. The kind of participation required in his work is not the joining in that characterized the audience-performer interactions of groups like the Living Theatre, nor the acceptance of a role with which the audience has been endowed, as in Grotowski's experiments. Boal's work demands that the audience assumes responsibility, makes judgements, and takes action on the basis of this judgement. The spect-actor does not remain merely an extra nor an additional protagonist, but becomes an amalgam of playwright, participant, and adjudicator. The spectators are no longer absolved from liability for what takes place on the stage. If necessary, they must be prepared to reconstruct, transform, and transcend the roles, situations, and events that they encounter.

If spectators in the theatre can become performers without losing detachment, participants in process drama can be changed into observers without abandoning involvement. The traditional lines of engagement are redrawn. Spectators act, and actors look on. Both functions are capable of coexistence.

Unity and Ambivalence

Although some of the spectators may take on the functions of the actors in Boal's work, they do not cease to function as members of an audience. They are united in their attention to and responsibility for providing and testing solutions to the problems before them. This unity is implicit in the definition of an audience. One of the major tasks for all theatre workers is to create this unity, because until the spectators are unified into an audience, they cannot effectively engage with the work. The shared social context in which spectators come together is one of the factors that creates in individuals a need to be at one with the work and with each other. Social contagion operates to create pressure toward group conformity, agreement, and acceptance.

The greatest uniformity of response has been shown to occur most strongly when ambivalence of feeling is the prevalent individual response. Ambivalence is an inevitable element in improvised drama—a product of the need to inhabit two worlds simultaneously.

Theatre produces the same effect. The audience's response to the actor is always profoundly ambivalent. If the spectators reject this ambivalence and treat the actor on stage as an ordinary person, they are refusing to acknowledge the nature of the theatre event.

In performance the boundaries between the real and the imaginary become blurred. We see a real actor inhabiting a fictitious world. As both the familiar and the unfamiliar are present in the actor, so both recognition and uneasiness are present in our response. What ought to reassure us, our knowledge that the actor is only pretending, merely creating an illusion, and, however mysterious, is also a real person, is precisely what troubles us most.

Playwrights and directors in all eras have exploited the kind of ambivalence and uneasiness that can be achieved by deliberately obscuring the boundaries between actors and audience, between illusion and reality. In Beaumont and Fletcher's *Knight of the Burning Pestle,* the Grocer and his wife, apparently part of the audience, invade the stage and demand a new play, one that will feature the adventures of their favorite apprentice, Ralph. Some years ago, a production of *The Taming of the Shrew* by the Royal Shakespeare Company at Stratford began with an apparently drunken spectator who climbed on stage and broke up the set, to the horror of the audience. Brook's *Oedipus Rex* blurred the line between performers and audience and achieved maximum unease by scattering the Chorus among the spectators to breathe, sigh, and howl at disconcertingly close quarters. Even one of the most venerable stage techniques, direct address, reaches across the footlights and makes the spectators acutely conscious of themselves in the darkness. Unease and ambivalence are likely to be heightened and resistance provoked in any situation where the spectators themselves are asked to enter and take responsibility for creating the illusion, whether this invitation occurs in the theatre or in improvised drama in the studio or classroom; it is this resistance that can lead to the collapse of the imagined world. In setting up the invitations or lures by which the participants are led into the action and encouraged to submit to the power of the dramatic world, the leader needs to employ an impressive range of skills and insights.

Return from Space

In this process drama, the element of watching is significant. It occurs in a number of the episodes and provides a powerful tension within the work.

•••

The teacher begins with narration. "In the twenty-first century, space exploration became a regular occurrence. Spaceships journeyed to the farthest corners of the galaxy. Not all of them returned. One such ship was the Starship Omega. Its mission was to travel to the edge of the galaxy. Unfortunately, it was caught in a meteor storm, and all contact with the ship was lost. It was listed as missing, and as the years went by, it was presumed lost forever."

Out of role, the teacher tells the group that they are psychiatrists and have been summoned urgently to the headquarters of NASA.

Episodes	Drama Elements
In role as a NASA official, the teacher thanks the group for responding so promptly to the urgent call for their services. She reminds them of the spaceship Omega and its loss fifteen years previously. Now, however, it has reappeared. The crew have been caught in a time field, and although they have all survived, there is a problem. Not only have they been posted as missing, presumed dead, but none of them is any older. They are not aware of how much time has actually passed.	The teacher's tone is serious and concerned. Only the psychiatrists can help the astronauts adjust to their new situation. This professional role allows the participants as a group to examine the implications of these circumstances. They are able to speculate about the loss suffered by the astronauts' families so long ago and how things might have changed.
The task is for the psychiatrists to break the news to the astronauts that fifteen years have passed and that their families have presumed that they are dead.	Building the dramatic world is a complex process, because the astronauts know nothing about their former histories, let alone how these may have changed.
Working in **Forum Theatre**, the official suggests that they examine possible ways of breaking the news. Two volunteers try out the interaction. The participants give suggestions on how best to proceed.	There is an important element of **watching** in this episode, although because it is a **rehearsal,** the spectators may intervene in the interaction.

Before the work proceeds, each member of the group is asked to imagine that he or she is on the spaceship returning to earth. They glimpse the earth beneath them, circled in clouds. Each writes a brief poem or diary entry on the subject of "home."

Next, working in pairs—one as astronaut, the other as psychiatrist—all the participants try out this encounter.

The psychiatrists meet with the NASA official and discuss the responses of the crew members. Some had difficulty accepting the situation. All were concerned about their families and the effect of their return on them.

In order to help them come to terms with what has happened, it is decided that the astronauts should view TV news items about the disappearance of their spaceship. In small groups, the participants choose a timeframe for their news item. These include the first news of the spaceship's disappearance, a memorial service, the first anniversary of its disappearance, the fifth anniversary, and so on.

The NASA official next meets with the astronauts while the psychiatrists are present. Their return is still a closely guarded secret. How should their families be told of their return?

The official offers a temporary solution. NASA has been monitoring the families and can share a videotape with each of the astronauts that will show the family's present state of affairs.

The groups "create" the videotape for four or five of the participants who have chosen to stay in role as astronauts. Each astronaut watches the videotape, while the rest of the

The participants are allowed to choose which role they would like to assume. Some may remain in these roles for the remainder of the drama.

The astronauts are **audience** to this feedback. Their responses in the previous episode are recalled and interpreted by the psychiatrists.

Once again, **watching** is a key part of this episode. There is a **public** quality to the presentations, which include both officials and politicians, but there is also a **private** dimension, as the families and friends grieve for their loved ones. Some of these presentations have a strong sense of **ritual**.

There is some hostility and suspicion in this interaction. The teacher in role as the NASA official is challenged about the government's apparent efforts to keep the matter quiet.

The astronauts agree to view these tapes, although they are uneasy about the covert surveillance that is implied.

Until now, half of the group has been in role as astronauts at several moments in the drama. Now they are allowed to choose whether they group, once more in role as psychiatrists, watches the astronaut watching the video.

These videos showed some partners recently remarried or falling in love, the death of elderly parents, and young adults choosing to follow their parents' heroic example and become astronauts. Some families were happy in their new lives; others were in crisis.

The official asks them for their decisions. Will they go back? How is this return to be managed? Those who choose not to return will be given a new identity. Each astronaut makes a decision.

Then, working with the group that earlier created the videotape, they create tableaux that reveal their decisions. In some, the astronaut has been reunited with the family; in others, they remain on the outside, looking in; in another, the astronaut has made a new life.

want to proceed in these roles, bearing in mind that they may be quite stressful.

This episode, a particularly complex kind of **watching**, was full of tension and emotion, yet distanced by the very fact of the astronauts' being on the outside of the proceedings.

This interaction involves only the five astronauts and the NASA official. The other participants are an **audience.**

This last activity is once again composed and prepared, and the groups are **audience** to the others' work. These **tableaux** allow for a variety of endings.

In a final, reflective phase, each participant chooses a piece of writing by another member of the group. Selecting a sentence, phrase, or word from this piece, the participants create a spontaneous collage entitled "Home." In the light of what we have seen in the drama, this becomes a poignant, ironic, and ambiguous commentary on the drama.

This process drama includes a particularly complex mixture of improvised encounters and composed episodes. The direct interactions with the psychiatrists and the NASA official were mostly discussion, yet the experience was not any less tense or moving for the participants because of this. In fact, the pervasive elements of watching seemed to allow for a greater degree of feeling in the group, as the participants explored notions of control and disclosure, home and belonging.

Dual Functions in Process Drama

The double stance of the participant-observer, or in Boal's term *spect-actor,* is recognized in educational drama by Bolton's term *percipient.* The quality of detached involvement that this word indicates will not necessarily arise of itself. An awareness of oneself and others as performers on some level is as necessary for process drama as it is for theatre. An action is defined as theatre not by its reality but by the state of mind of the person who performs it.

Meanings must be communicated and understood, and this can occur only through publicly performed words and actions. Bolton has characterized dramatic playing as containing for the participants both the feeling that "this is happening to me" and "I am making it happen."[15] In this formulation, the sense of being a spectator to what one is creating remains functional and implicit. A stronger sense of audience would add a third dimension—"I am watching this happening to me, and I am making it happen." Like Foreman's description of the active audience, the task for those involved in process drama is to be in two places at once. They see, and they see themselves seeing.[16]

There is a growing understanding of the essential nature of this audience function. Both Bolton and Heathcote have strengthened the elements of reflection and contemplation in their work and have begun to recharacterize the participants as both actors and audience. This trend has been in the opposite direction from that of avant-garde theatre, which sought to make spectators into performers. In education, the shift has been to recognize the limitations of the notion that improvised drama is "doing," and to alter the participants' sphere of action from being performers to functioning within the action with a certain degree of objectivity as active observers. To achieve this shift, a degree of distance is required in the roles with which the participants are endowed. They have to be placed at a certain distance from the action, psychologically and physically, before they can see it.

Teacher in Role

Several particular strategies are implicated in the participants' change of perspective from an emphasis on action toward a more objective stance. The first, teacher in role, is, in fact, rather more than a strategy. This complex tactic, touched on earlier, in which the teacher or leader initiates the dramatic world by adopting a role, offers both a change of stance to the teacher or leader and an opportunity to function as playwright within the work. It is important here to examine its operation as a means of engaging participants in active contemplation and inviting them to live in both the real and the imagined world.

Teacher in role operates to focus the attention of the participants, harness their feelings of ambivalence and vulnerability, unite them in contemplation, and engage them in action. There is the beginning of a kind of "audience mind," which is affirmed in perception and response. Like the theatre audience, the participants in process drama are caught up in a complex pattern of expectation and reaction. They begin to "read" the performance of the teacher in role, searching for clues about the dramatic world that is being born before their eyes. Among the clues for which they will be searching is a sense of their own relationship to the teacher's role, their own role function, and the power and possibility it presents. They become united in paying attention to the fiction created by the teacher in role. In Heathcote's phrase, they have permission to stare. The teacher in role is engaged in an act of conscious self-presentation, but one that casts the watchers in functional roles, invites them to respond actively, to join in, and if necessary, to oppose and transform what is happening. From within the dramatic world that is being evoked, the teacher or leader can manipulate language and gesture to establish the nature of this world. Criteria of possibility are established, appropriate conventions are seen in action, a sense of genre is developed, and the likely range of the action is suggested.

Tableaux

The strategy, variously labeled "depiction," "tableau," "frozen picture," or "freeze frame," has been enormously valuable in enabling those working in process drama to strengthen the reflective element in their work. It is included in several of the examples provided in this book. An image of some kind is prepared and presented, typically by a small group, to the rest of the participants. Strictly speaking, this kind of activity is not improvised spontaneously, but this will not invalidate it as part of the process.

> In a sense, all art is improvisation. Some improvisations are presented "as is," whole and at once; others are doctored improvisations that have been revised and restructured over a period of time before the public gets to enjoy the work. A composer who writes on paper is still improvising to begin with, if "only" men-

tally, then taking the products of the improvisation and refining and applying technique to them.[17]

The function of a tableau is to arrest attention, to detain the viewers, to impede their perception. Tableau or depiction has a long history in both educational drama and theatre. For Diderot, and later Brecht, the perfect play is a succession of tableaux, a series of segmentations each of which possesses a sufficient demonstrative power.[18] It has been a dominant structure in the work of such innovative artists as Stein, Godard, Glass, Foreman, and Wilson. As well as possessing demonstrative power, a tableau has the multiple function of compelling the spectator to analyze its specific placement in the artistic framework, of framing or throwing a scene into relief, and of stopping or expanding time.

> The stillness of tableaux sequences suspends time, causing the
> eye to focus on an image and slows down the process of input.
> This increases the critical activity of the mind. It regulates the dia-
> lectical interplay of word and image.[19]

The image arrests and detains us and commands our attention and interpretation. There is more in the tableau than a mere suspension of time. The "perfect instant" of the tableau is both totally concrete and totally abstract. In it we can read at a single glance the present, the past, and the future—in other words the complete meaning of the represented action.

In both theatre and process drama, the significance of the use of a tableau lies in its expansion of the participants' capacity to perceive. It is both significant and reflexive. A frozen image will compel the observers to interrogate it for its possible meanings. Even when used at the beginning or end of a play, as in Ibsen's *Ghosts,* it forces a question on us.

The selective use of a tableau as a unit of activity within process drama releases participants from the demands of action, requires deliberate composition, embodies understanding, manifests meaning, allows time to be frozen or recalled, permits a level of abstraction to enter the work, and shapes and shares both information and insight. A tableau can operate almost as a play within a play and can reflect or criticize the apparent values of the work, rather like the "shows" that Prospero provides in *The Tempest* or the dumbshow Hamlet inserts into his Mousetrap. Wherever devices of this kind are used, the effect is to implicate the spectators as voyeurs and to heighten their consciousness of their dual function as participants and critical observers.

Forum Theatre

Boal's strategy of inviting spectators to enter and transform the action, which he calls "Forum Theatre," can also be effectively employed within the structure of process drama. In this case, the situation is improvised, but it is an improvisation that can be halted, modified, and transformed by the spect-actors or "percipients." It may be more accurate to think of this procedure, like tableaux, as a kind of composition. Composition is not necessarily the opposite of improvisation. Schoenberg has described composing as a "slowed-down" improvisation.[20] Forum Theatre appears to expose the performers but actually protects them by their primary stance as audience. They remain free to feel without the danger of exposure, while taking responsibility for the dramatic behavior of those engaged in the interaction. Those members of the group who have volunteered to take on roles in the scene are also protected, because they are not required to improvise freely. They are standing in for the rest of the spectators, and much of their dialogue, gestures, actions, and decisions may be provided by the audience, although they may also be free to contribute to the scene. The entire group, including both actors and audience, exercises control over what is taking place in terms of image, gesture, action, and language; it manipulates the staging and makes decisions about spatial relationships within the mise-en-scene.

When tableaux, forum theatre, and other prepared and presented episodes are part of a developing process drama, the participants are not merely *composing* images or scenes with particular dramatic characteristics, but simultaneously *apprehending* them in their formal and structural relationships. These episodes enlarge the emergent meaning of the work and encourage both reflection and extension.

Assistance

"Necessary theatre," according to Brook, is that in which audiences feel the same compulsive necessity as that felt by theatre workers. Interestingly, the only true image of necessary theatre that Brook provides is that of a psychodrama session in an asylum. He notes that two hours after any session begins, all of the relationships among the people present are modified because of the experience they have shared. When they leave the room, they are not the same as when they entered. These conditions, which Brook tries to create in theatre, can be found in a successful process drama. There, too, relationships can be modified, understandings achieved, and significant experiences shared.

Brook proposes the use of a most valuable French word, *assistance,* in outlining the function of the ideal theatre audience. In French, "I watch a play" translates into "J'assiste a une piece." In English, the function of the congregation at a religious ceremony is to "assist" at the event. This term helps to clarify the activities and attitudes that are likely to strengthen reflection and contemplation in process drama. An audience that brings an active interest to the theatre event assists at the performance.

> Representation no longer separates actor and audience, show and public: it envelops them: what is present for one is present for the other. The audience too has undergone change. It has come from a life outside the theatre . . . to a special arena in which each moment is lived more clearly and more tensely. The audience assists the actor and at the same time, for the audience, assistance comes back from the stage.[21]

In other innovative art forms, and in particular the novel, it has been recognized that an active, conscious, creative assistance is required from readers or spectators. There is seldom a complete and ready-made world to be received; instead, spectators participate in a creation, and help to invent the work.

We learn from theatre and process drama because they are fictions, actively co-created and, in the case of process drama, actively entered. Where involvement in the action predominates, the reflective element is necessarily weakened. A truly engaged yet detached aesthetic response is more demanding than total involvement, but anything less is scarcely worth attempting. The art work is a "field for noticing," and Foreman insists that the only justifiable technique in art that is not simply audience manipulation is to learn how to be in two places at once, "both seeing and seeing yourself seeing."[22]

The notion of dramatic action that can be observed, held up for examination, and investigated for the truths it may contain will operate as an invaluable principle of selection in structuring process drama. But there is a danger that the very usefulness of such approaches as tableaux and forum theatre may subvert the essentially improvised nature of the work. In some cases, drama teachers have become overdependent on strategies of this kind and, in particular, on the use of tableaux. They offer a safe and apparently purposeful task for participants, do not necessarily require technical skills, and are easily set up by the teacher. The mere fact of setting up such a task, however, will not necessarily result in reflection or elaboration. Without encouragement and the deliberate adoption of an interpretive stance, the task will not modify or extend the experience of the drama. Even where participants are encouraged to "read" the results of this task, a further danger may be that the dramatic action is submerged in composition and contemplation. Spontaneous improvisatory interactions and encounters are crucial in creating the dramatic world in action and driving the event forward. It is important not to neglect the spontaneous encounter of improvised dramatic action in favor of composing depicted images or abstractions. Too great a swing in the process from action to reflection may mean that nothing remains to be contemplated.

Engagement and Detachment

Each of the three approaches outlined here offers the possibility of an engaged yet detached response within improvised drama. There is not merely action, but also contemplation. Participants are caught up in the development of the imagined world, but because of the need to maintain and articulate this world, a certain detachment is a necessity. Responsibility for what is taking place is diffused among the participants, who take on part of the playwright function and who may simultaneously or sequentially be performers and spectators. Each strategy establishes an occurrence that demands to be "read" actively and compels observation as well as involvement.

Where process drama is structured so that there is a significant public dimension as well as the need for reflection, and where the participants' sense of being both actors and audience is actively promoted, the dramatic world will be built on a powerful and effective combination of dramatic action and active contemplation.

Devices: Structuring the Dramatic Experience

■ **Those who accept** the validity of process drama as a significant dramatic experience and wish to explore this exciting form face considerable challenges. They will require the ability to

- select an effective pre-text
- decide on roles for the leader and the participants
- sequence the scenic units or episodes
- determine their temporal dimension and their place in the process
- choose the mode of activity for each episode

In earlier chapters I suggested a range of guiding principles, but there are further key questions to be addressed. What specific dramatic forms can be drawn on to give substance to the process? What kinds of encounter will yield the most significant experience for the participants in each episode? How can the leader build a framework that is sufficiently flexible to allow each participant to engage in a satisfyingly complex role? How can the group come to take an increasing share in the essential playwright function and make decisions about the direction of the work? The best guide for both leader and participants in process drama is a strong sense of dramatic form, a grasp of the structural devices by which playwrights through the ages have created significant dramatic experience, and an understanding of the relationship of content to form in the work.

Whether in traditional or contemporary theatre practice, the dramatists' possibilities for action are not unlimited. The same kinds of dramatic action and encounter have been exploited repeatedly throughout the history of the drama, and these can be used with equal force in process drama. Among the devices that have proved to have enduring utility are watching, inquiry, games and contests, appearances, roles within roles, public and private dimensions, and rituals. All of these have a place in process drama.

Macbeth

In order to establish that process drama can contain the same kinds of formal features and structural devices that occur in classic drama, it is helpful to examine the operation of these features in a classic play. I have chosen *Macbeth,* one of the most compact of Shakespeare's works. My objective is not to equate the achievement of a great play with an ephemeral and improvised process, but is to discover similar structural elements at work in both.

Episodes	Drama Elements
Shakespeare's pre–pre-text is the account in Holinshed of the career of the usurper, Macbeth. In the actual play, the first scene with the witches operates as a pre-text, a kind of "holding form," that anticipates the encounters to come.	This **pre-text** indicates the genre and some of the power relationships that will be established. The first scene sets the **atmosphere** of evil and raises questions and **expectations**.
The second scene, the aftermath of the battle, gives us the context, the social setting, and perspectives on Macbeth and provides us with more information than Macbeth himself possesses—the news of the death of Cawdor and the gift of his titles to Macbeth.	Narration, exposition, explanation, and expectation confirm the violent events of the recent **past** and **reaches toward the future**. There is a sense of **audience**, a **public** quality. Comments about Macbeth already have an ironic effect because the real audience is now more knowledgeable than the protagonists.
We meet Macbeth only in the third scene, when the victorious generals are confronted by the witches. Here Banquo might almost be mistaken for the hero of the play, if we didn't know better, as he and Macbeth receive the witches' salutations and predictions.	The main action of the play is set in motion by the prediction that Macbeth will be King "hereafter." The actors are **audience**, commenting and making judgements on the action. We begin to judge them by their responses.
Once the Macbeths discuss their "former thoughts" about killing the king, the expectations that we have	The **past** is hinted by implication. The Macbeths begin the process of **concealment** that will undo them.

been developing begin to grow. The intimate and **private** nature of this scene make us, as audience, almost co-conspirators.

External action is balanced by revelations of their interior life.

With King Duncan's arrival at Dunsinane, the change of mood allows us to savor both the powerful irony that suffuses the scene and Lady Macbeth's consummate skill in deception, in looking like "the innocent flower," but being the serpent under it.

Here, in a **public** and **ceremonial** setting, there is sharp irony, **roleplaying within the role**, and **tension**. The tension builds through the sequence of scenes that lead up to and include the murder.

The Macbeths carry out their plot in a series of brief scenes of almost unbearable tautness, achieved through repetition and accumulation.

We are not only caught up in their crime, but are almost inside their heads, as they give us glimpses of their thoughts through their soliloquies.

The function of the drunken porter has been much discussed, but certainly operates as a powerful contrast and release. It is worth noting the "performances" of the Macbeths after the discovery of Duncan. Their behavior is being narrowly studied by the rest of the court, as they enact their dismay and horror.

His rambling commentary allows a **decrease in tension** and a change of tone from the terrible intensity of the murder's aftermath. There is an **audience** to the Macbeths' **display** of grief, and one that is not fully convinced of the sincerity of the performance.

The tiny scene with Ross and the Old Man allows us further contemplation in order to reflect on the unnatural events of the night and place them in the context of the Old Man's "threescore and ten."

This scene allows **contemplation, reflection** and **foreboding**. It gives a breathing space in the onward rush of events, and the horror of the murder and its implications sinks in.

In the next few scenes Macbeth struggles to maintain his security by arranging the murder of Banquo and his son. We see his struggles to win against the Fate which seemed to grant him the crown, but now denies him the future enjoyment of it.

There is a powerful sense of **future** considerations ruling Macbeth's actions. We begin to be distanced from him, as he no longer ponders the morality of his acts, and see him begin to wade in blood.

At the banquet, the central and most powerful scene in the play, the guests are reduced to the status of audience to Macbeth's increasingly bizarre behavior. They have no influence on what happens and merely note the events in front of them, although Lady Macbeth, at least, is powerfully aware of their presence. Macbeth, the business-like murderer, falls to pieces before our eyes.

The element of **audience** is important here, as we see both **public and private** aspects of the Macbeths. Lady Macbeth is still capable of public **roleplaying**. The **appearance** of Banquo's ghost is the pivot on which the scene turns. There is a compulsively predictable repetition and escalation of events in the scene.

The scene with Lennox which follows is a savagely ironic commentary on the preceding murders— "Men must not walk too late"—as well as hinting at hope for the future, in Macduff's denial of Macbeth's summons.

Again, a brief linking scene has a vital function in allowing **reflection, contemplation,** and savage irony.

On Macbeth's return to the witches, he becomes an audience of one to his own future, which they unfold before him in a series of tableaux.

This scene has almost the force of a **play within the play**. Macbeth is **audience** to an occult **ritual.**

The supernatural horror of this scene is in powerful contrast to the peaceful domestic setting that culminates in the most visible malevolence in the play, the murder of Macduff's "pretty chickens and their dam."

The **contrast** between Macbeth's evil and the innocence of his victims continues the process of **distancing** us from identification with him. The precocious reflections of the child provide an ironic counterpoint.

The long scene between Macduff and Malcolm in the English court is not merely a sharp change of pace and location but also moves our attention both backward and forward in time. The cure for "Scotland's woes" must originate from outside.

Malcolm plays a kind of confidence **trick** on Macduff by falsely representing his own behavior. This is the first **test** of Macduff's character in the scene; the second is the news of his family's murder.

Lady Macbeth's dream, as well as being a riveting dramatic moment, includes a number of significant

This is a powerful use of the **dream**, our last glimpse of Lady Macbeth's tormented mind, in front structural features. The scene takes place with a concealed audience, the Doctor and the Nurse, as she reenacts in an unbearably attenuated way the terrible events to which she was a witness.

The onward rush of retribution overtakes Macbeth, and he finds no time to mourn his wife's suicide. We glimpse his thoughts through his terse soliloquies. His recognition that he has lost everything that makes life worth living—"honor, love, obedience, troops of friends"—descends to the despair of "a tale told by an idiot, full of sound and fury, signifying nothing."

These backward glances are repeated in the final scene. After Macbeth's death at the hands of Macduff, in spite of the witches' promises, there is an anticipation of the future stability and prosperity of Scotland under Duncan's true heir, Malcolm.

of **eavesdroppers**, informed professionals whose comments carry weight. There is reenactment, repetition, and recapitulation.

Macbeth's soliloquies provide moments of **contemplation** in the midst of action; there is a powerful sense of the **past** and vanished dreams of the **future**. He begins to recognize just how thoroughly the Witches have **tricked** him with "honest trifles" and betrayed him.

At long last, Macbeth, "tied to the stake," refuses to live to be a common spectacle, and we witness his defeat. The play ends **ceremonially**, with a final glance at past and future.

In this brief summary of some of the structural qualities of *Macbeth,* I have highlighted several features that will be particularly helpful to remember when attempting to structure process drama. These dramatic features and devices are used by playwrights again and again, as they devise occasions and situations in which their characters can encounter and interact with each other. Characters in drama make announcements, bring news, narrate events, question, persuade, plead, accuse, judge, and quarrel with each other. They play tricks, tell jokes, engage in physical contests and battles of wits, sing, dance, pray, curse, threaten, praise and blame, prophesy, and mourn, and do all of these things and more in a variety of ways. In process drama, all these possibilities are available to the participants and may be selected as key actions in particular episodes of the dramatic structure.

Pre-text

I want to recall here some of the characteristics of the key notion of **pre-text** that were covered in more detail earlier. A decision must be made as to the starting point of any process drama, as well as its possible theme, location, or genre because the playwright function cannot operate in a vacuum. Sometimes these decisions are made by the participants and sometimes by the leader. They may be as sketchy as a wish to explore the supernatural or to visit outer space, or a more precise pre-text may be chosen by either leader and/or participants.

At one time, I believed that almost *any* material or stimulus could be used as a springboard for exploration. It has become obvious to me that pre-texts must be selected very carefully. Not all potential pre-texts will easily evoke a dramatic world. The pre-text must be chosen, not just for the kind of story, theme, or issue it contains, but also for specific characteristics. These include

- its responsiveness to imaginative transformation
- the tensions, changes, or contrasts it suggests
- the questions it raises about identity and society, power and possibility
- its power to launch the dramatic world with economy and clarity, propose action, and imply transformation

An effective pre-text is simple and functional. It sets in motion situations in which appearance and reality, truth and deception, and role and identity may be contrasted and explored. It is likely to provide an introduction to the work or to be, in effect, the first scene or episode of the drama.

A simple but effective pre-text arose not from a classic play, as in earlier examples, but from a play title. A colleague recommended that I read a rarely performed play by Farquhar, *Love in a Bottle*. I couldn't find a copy of this unfamiliar play, but the title intrigued me. It seemed like an economical starting point for process drama. Working with a group of highschool students, I began in role without any explanations. I told the group that I felt we should congratulate ourselves. After seven years of hard work in the laboratory, we had finally been successful. We'd achieved our aim and synthesized a wonderful substance. Here it was, I announced, indicating a small vial filled with liquid—"Love in a Bottle."

It became apparent that we were scientists who'd been working secretly on this task. We reflected on some of the key moments in our search, of both delight and despair. Now, we'd reached the point where we had to test the substance more widely. We knew it was not toxic but were unsure about its more precise properties. Working in groups, the students decided the kinds of tests they were going to administer, bearing in mind that only a very small amount of the substance was available. Then they presented TV news items that showed, in some cases indirectly, the results of the secret tests. These were both hilarious and moving. As the work progressed, it led to investigation and reflection on the nature of different kinds of love and the accountability and ethics of scientists. The pre-text had worked effectively to launch the world of scientists and their discoveries, as I'd hoped. Later I discovered that I had misheard the original title of the play, which is, in fact, *Love and a Bottle.* It seems to me that the misunderstanding provided me with a more serviceable pretext than the real name of the play.

Beginning in the Middle

An effective pre-text allows the dramatic world to come into existence with an immediacy that is characteristic of the most effective theatre pieces. In launching *Troilus and Cressida,* Shakespeare does not spend time repeating all the causes and details of the Trojan War. Instead, the essential facts are listed by the Prologue, which announces that

> [O]ur play
> Leaps o'er the vaunt and firstlings of those broils,
> Beginning in the middle; starting then away
> To what may be digested as a play.

To begin in the middle is good advice for the leader in process drama. Sometimes a great deal of time is spent preparing participants to enter the world of the drama. Games, trust exercises, and brief improvisations may be used to create the climate of consensus and community in which the dramatic world can take root or in which time may be spent on research and instruction about the theme. These activities can be valuable in focusing the minds of the participants on a particular theme, providing information, or beginning to establish the atmosphere of the drama. It may not be necessary to include separate warm-up activities. Process drama may be introduced in ways that are both initiatory and powerfully dramatic. An example of an introductory activity that achieves a number of complex effects is the ritual of molding an imaginary doll, used by Gavin Bolton when *The Crucible* was his pre-text. It initiated the work and resonated throughout the action in much the same way as the meeting of the witches on the blasted heath sets the tone of *Macbeth*. The initial episodes of the *Red Riding Hood* drama are also preparatory and realize several key objectives for the leader. On the other hand, it may be just as effective to plunge straight into the first episode of the drama and lead the participants directly across the threshold of the dramatic world, a world that is realized only as they enter it.

Moments of Change

Great dramatists typically waste little time in lengthy exposition in order to establish the nature of the dramatic world as it has been before the play begins. This world may be described to us or we may deduce what it was like, but the playwright is likely to present it to us at a moment of change, rather than allowing us to savor it in the fullness of its existence. Instead, the first scenes will swiftly introduce the key characters and their relationships, sketch potential lines of tension, and provide most economically the mood and genre of the piece. We must grasp the essential features of the world as rapidly and fully as possible, before it begins to alter forever. This moment of change is likely to be marked by a significant event. The kinds of events that signal this change and have proved dramatically effective in all eras include arrivals, encounters, returns, questions, proclamations, announcements of new laws, prophecies, and messages.

Arrivals make for an immediate change in the equilibrium of the dramatic world—as for example, Christy Mahon in *The Playboy of the Western World* and Blanche in *A Streetcar Named Desire*. *Returns* are equally powerful—the Ghost in *Hamlet* and Hedda and (later) Eilat Lovborg in *Hedda Gabler*. *Questions* and *messages* can launch the world—King Lear's question to his daughters, news of Desdemona's marriage to Othello and of the return of Agamemnon from Troy, and the witches' greeting to Macbeth.

In process drama it is possible to use exactly these same keys to the doors of the dramatic worlds we want the participants to enter. Beginning with an arrival, for example, precipitates the kinds of encounters that define the development of the drama. Refugees arriving in a new country may be greeted by an apparently sympathetic official, the leader in role, who gradually reveals the kinds of discrimination and segregation that the immigrants will face. Space travelers' reaching an unknown planet encounter an alien. The refusal of this alien to accept the fact that male crew members could be in positions of authority brings about a questioning of the power that attaches to gender roles and may lead to the creation and exploration of an imagined society in which females are dominant.[1] A return is another kind of arrival. In *Frank Miller,* the return of Frank creates tension and expectation and precipitates the action of the drama.

Asking the right kind of question, and asking it in role, is also an effective means of bringing new worlds into being. The introduction to *The Haunted House* lesson, in *Drama Structures,* sets up a challenge that is hard to ignore. The teacher in role as the ambiguous Mrs. Brown asks the students, "Will you spend one night in Darkwood House for $100?" This question, authenticated through the newspaper advertisement in which it is supposed to appear, operates as a pre-text that brings the world into being, establishes the genre, and provides a task that, like Hamlet's task of revenge at another level, may take a considerable time to achieve.[2]

Narration

Narrative and dramatic structure are very different in their operation and effects. Nevertheless, narration can be used effectively within a process drama. Shakespeare uses it sparingly as a device for very particular purposes—to change the physical setting and move on in time (*Henry V*), to furnish essential background information on situation (*The Tempest*) or character (*Macbeth*), to allow an ironic or poignant commentary on the main action (*As You Like It* and *Othello*), or to provide links between episodes in an extended plot structure (*Pericles*). Sometimes the narrator is defined as a storyteller or Chorus; sometimes a character will be given the task of providing essential background information or ironic commentary to the action in the form of a story. Narrative segments are often embedded dramatically in linking scenes such as that between Lennox and "another Lord," in which they reflect ironically on the murderous deeds of Macbeth and tell of Macduff's mission to the court of King Edward.

Too great a dependence on narration in either theatre or process drama may reveal an incompetence or uncertainty in dealing with the material, a need to control or limit the response of the audience or participants, or it may expose the unsuitability of the material for dramatic transformation. An example of the overuse of narration appears in Shaffer's *Yonadab,* in my opinion a clumsily structured and hollowly pretentious play. Excessive reliance on narration will reduce dramatic impact, destroy the sense of an unfolding present tense, and turn the event from the mode of destiny to the mode of history. Narration also may be contained effectively in songs outside of the dramatic action but commenting on it, as in Brecht's *Caucasian Chalk Circle.*

As I showed earlier, process drama may contain both improvisation and composition. Improvisation is spontaneous, absorbing, and dynamic. Composition is symmetrical and contains the tension of opposites. When these modes are combined in a process drama, the resulting event will have wholeness and integrity, as well as a sense of economy, consistency, completeness, and open-endedness in its organization. We may not always be able to define these qualities precisely, but we will readily recognize them in operation.

Games

As in theatre, actual games may be included in the dramatic structure. Their purpose is not to "warm up" participants nor develop trust or concentration, but to function structurally and thematically. They are not likely to be included at the beginning of the drama, because few games will have the capacity to launch a dramatic world effectively, but may occur later at a significant point in the drama. They will serve to recall an earlier moment and express it in an alternative form, to heighten tension, and to introduce or recall the feeling qualities of the theme. They provide a change of pace and a tightening or slackening of tension. They are particularly useful in picking up the work again if some time has intervened between sessions.

Many great plays, both tragic and comic, include games and contests. These can be dramatic in themselves and offer valuable opportunities for competition and display. The wrestling match in *As You Like It,* the fencing contest in *Hamlet,* the chess game in *The Tempest,* the card games and conjuring in Chekhov's plays, the battles of wits between Beatrice and Benedick, all have a structural function. Contemporary playwrights, from Brecht and Beckett to Albee and Mamet, recognize the usefulness of games. The judgement of Solomon episode in *The Caucasian Chalk Circle* and the game of "Get the Guests" in *Who's Afraid of Virginia Woolf?* are just two examples.

Many comedies are structured through the con game that characters play on unsuspecting dupes. In *Tartuffe, Volpone,* or *Twelfth Night* we watch these games run their course until the winners and losers are clearly known. In *Measure for Measure* the "bed trick" is played on Angelo to right a wrong, and in *The Changeling* to protect the wicked. The games that Iago and Richard III play with their victims are full of tension, especially as we, the spectators, are directly addressed and apparently recognized by these characters and are thereby implicated in their conspiracies. Puzzles, tests, and riddles are all structurally satisfying—for example, the riddle asked of Oedipus by the Sphinx or the choice of Portia's caskets. These devices are equally useful in process drama.

Elementary students in role as advisers to a great African king were given the task of selecting a bride for him. During the two-hour process drama that ensued, the students established criteria for selection of a bride, disguised their identities and went undercover, devised tests, answered riddles, and solved problems. After they had chosen a short list of candidates, they determined to choose the bride on the basis of her resourcefulness and usefulness to the people. The worst difficulty facing their country, they decided, was shortage of water. The leader presented the prospective brides with a problem.

They were asked to imagine that in front of them was an old woman, a baby, and a cow. If they had one pail of water, to whom would they give it? Neither the candidates nor the advisers could decide on the best answer to the riddle, but a tremendously lively debate ensued. Finally, further trials had to be set, including a final challenge to the candidates. They were told that the advisers had never, in fact, seen the king, who might not even prove to be human. Could they still face him?

Games and contests have a ritual quality that provides another kind of structured experience for the participants in process drama. "Hunter and Hunted," the game used in *Frank Miller,* helped to recall the tension associated with the event without recourse to merely retelling the story. It echoed themes of seeking and finding, of groping in the dark, of being pursued by an unknown predator that resonate in the drama. In *The Seal Wife,* the game of searching for a partner's hands was one of the most deeply felt episodes in the piece.

Watching

In process drama, where there is no separate audience, there is a need for the leader to "switch on the watcher" in the participants in order to achieve a balance of engagement and detachment. In the same way that Grotowski and other innovative theatre artists recharacterized their audiences as actors within the theatre event, so participants may be recharacterized in process drama as spectators. This implies something more dynamic than merely promoting an objective attitude to what is viewed within the work. It is possible for the element of watching to begin to function as a structural principle within the event. The leader in process drama can achieve this through the same means by which dramatists entrap their audiences in a web of watching. In theatre, the original equation of watchers and watched is likely to be further complicated and elaborated by the dramatist doubling and tripling the occasions of watching.

In *Hamlet*, the play within the play turns Claudius' court into an audience. But, while Claudius watches *The Mousetrap* and Hamlet watches Claudius, Rosencrantz and Guildenstern watch Hamlet, Horatio watches them and we, the spectators, watch all this watching. Spying and eavesdropping are essential features of the play. Laurence Olivier emphasized this in his film of *Hamlet*, with the camera sliding up and down staircases, glancing from behind pillars, and peeping in at casements. This kind of doubled watching is so common a feature of great drama that it acquires the force of a structural principle. Examples are as frequent in comedy as in tragedy—*Twelfth Night, The School for Scandal, The Duchess of Malfi, The Changeling,* and *Tartuffe,* among many others.

In process drama, watching as a structural feature can be employed from the outset through the roles with which the participants are endowed. Spies, detectives, investigators, journalists, psychiatrists, historians are all roles that imply action and have both the need and the right to watch closely, to pay attention, to re-create, and to interpret what is happening or what has already taken place. Like that of an audience in the theatre, these perspectives will bring with them tasks of detection and interpretation, both of which imply a detached objective stance. Psychiatrists will observe their client's behavior; spy-catchers will tap telephones; reporters will produce "scoops," make documentaries, and prepare reports; detectives will watch suspects through one-way mirrors and reconstruct crimes; archivists will examine records of earlier times to find the truth of past events. These are all highly dramatic activities, but the tasks involved will demand a certain physical and psychological distance. The urgency of the townspeople in *Frank Miller* was tempered by their need to observe the strangers in town closely for clues as to their real identities.

Inquiry

The theatre is a laboratory for witnessing and investigating what the British playwright Howard Barker calls "unlived life." The theatre is essentially hypothetical, built on such moral speculation as King Lear's question, "Is there any cause in Nature that make these hard hearts?" The theatre always asks, "Are we thus?" And it provides us with some of the answers. Trials and debates have been popular with dramatists of all periods, from *Oedipus Rex* to plays of the present day. Legal processes provide the heart of the work in *The Eumenides, The Merchant of Venice, Measure for Measure, St. Joan, The Crucible,* and countless other lesser plays.

Trials in real life are already deeply dramatic. They seek to discover the truth about a person or an incident, or, perhaps, to cover up that truth. Their purpose is disclosure, which implies a prior concealment, as well as an attempt to see things from a number of different perspectives. Certainly there is no better way of giving spectators a stake in the action and an actual task than to ask for their judgement—to require them to sift the evidence before them for the truths it may contain. According to Arthur Miller, the theatre will always be a form of jurisprudence.[3] Every variety of investigation—trials, inquiries, courts martial, interrogations—occurs throughout the history of the theatre and all imply the question, "Who's to blame?" Even where there is no actual legal process taking place, the interrogation of the past in order to come at the truth provides a powerful motivating force for the action in such plays as O'Neill's *Long Day's Journey into Night* or Miller's *The Price*. These processes are powerful structural elements that will operate as effectively in process drama as in a classic play. They contain implications of past and future and demand involvement at the same time that they require objectivity.

To ask "Who's to Blame?" in process drama will immediately structure the experience in a particular way and imply a series of actions and encounters. Drama as inquiry is one of the most straightforward, but also satisfying, forms to explore. The result of the inquiry is truly unknown, but the dramatic action is driven by a need to discover the truth about a person or an event. Interviews, interrogations, the collecting of evidence, tableaux recreating or speculating about past happenings, reconstructions of particular incidents, all provide material for the actual legal process. This may be a preliminary hearing, a trial by jury, a court martial, a kangaroo court, an illegal tribunal set up to administer justice of a particular kind, or the court of conscience, an inquiry taking place within the mind of the protagonist. In theatre, this latter kind of inquiry often occurs in the form of a dream, as in the accusations that Brutus faces in his tent before the battle of Phillipi or those of Richard III on Bosworth Field. The trial of *Frank Miller* took place in the past, but the injustice done to Frank in that corrupt court was the cause of his exile and eventual return. The question that was posed throughout the drama was not only "Who is Frank Miller?" but also "What has he become?"

Roles

When the roles adopted by participants in process drama become the object of inquiry, an essential structural principle of theatre is at work. Roles that are doubled or denied immediately give direction, tension, and complexity to the unfolding event. The hidden identity of Frank Miller and his secret purpose is what drives the work forward and brings what is concealed to light. In *The Seal Wife,* the impulse behind the drama is the fact that the wife is not what she seems. She belongs in another world. When an actor is required to role-play within the role, the task is an extremely precise one. It is easy to undertake this task in process drama—to play one role in order to conceal another. The audience works to discover the truth of the situation, and the role is perceived as having depth, ambiguity, and complexity.

When a character is clearly role-playing within a role, there are two tasks for the spectators' or participants' comprehension. The first is to recognize the role attributes that are being assumed, for example, those of king, trusted friend, virtuous young man, playboy, old aunt from Brazil. The second is to discern to what extent this role is being undermined, corrupted, or parodied. The effect of these efforts is to focus attention on the key attributes of both the original role that is being hidden or denied and the role that has been falsely assumed. As Lady Macbeth urges her husband to dissemble, we see both the innocent flower and the serpent under it. We have a clear task of judgement and interpretation that immediately strengthens our understanding of "noble" Macbeth and the "dead butcher" he becomes. Character is defined by its opposite, and the masks worn by those who are role-playing within their roles will paradoxically reveal much about their true natures. Role-playing within a role, in both theatre and process drama, exposes the very nature of role itself.

It is not only the character who hides or disappears behind another role. Actors and participants in process drama are also hidden, however momentarily, by any roles they may adopt. Protected and concealed by their roles within the dramatic world, they are at once both more and less than themselves. They embody both present meaning and future possibility. Theatre and process drama provide an experimental setting in which we can investigate questions of identity and explore both the power and the limitations of the roles that we may inhabit. This exploration of identity through roleplay and in particular, role-playing within a role, is, for me, at the heart of *all* drama. It is the single most powerful source of significant meaning in the work and the root of the dramatic action.

Appearances

To some extent, actors who stand before us on the stage are *appearances*. We encounter a paradox—something that is real and not real at the same time. Like the element of watching, this disturbing quality can also be doubled. It is no wonder that playwrights through the ages have presented ghosts and spirits to our view. Their appearances both authenticate and undermine the reality of the actor. The spirits of his murdered foes who torment Richard III on Bosworth field, Banquo's ghost, Hamlet's father, the population of the graveyard in *Our Town,* and the vengeful first wife in *Blithe Spirit* are among those ghosts who return from the grave with a clear purpose. Other appearances have a different kind of reality for the characters who encounter them, and may be evil or benign. They are visions of a different order—the line of kings conjured up by the witches in *Macbeth*, Prospero's masque, Faustus' angels and devils, and all the disembodied voices of the drama carrying messages of hope or despair. One of the most poignant is the Echo in *The Duchess of Malfi,* which speaks in the voice of the murdered Duchess, "a dead thing," and foreshadows to Antonio the outcome of the tragedy. Sometimes, disembodied voices arise from within the mind of the protagonist, but are actual appearances on stage, such as Willy Loman's brother from Alaska. Brian Friel, in *Philadelphia Here I Come,* actually divided his main character into inner and outer voices, both embodied on stage but only one visible to the other characters, with both painful and hilarious consequences.

In process drama, it is possible to show these inner and outer voices. In a process drama based on *Dr. Faustus,* our versions of the Good and Bad Angels became the voices of Faustus' conscience, played by two other participants alternately urging him on and attempting to restrain him. In *The Seal Wife,* the fisherman was surrounded by the voices of his wife and children as they accused, blamed, comforted, and tormented him.

Dreams

The dream, although not always an actual experience, is a device that is similar to and equally popular as the inner voice. The dream fulfills several important purposes for the dramatist. It allows glimpses into the minds of the characters in a way that extends our knowledge of them beyond their outward behaviors. Dreams perform several functions, including the foreshadowing of coming events, as in Calpurnia's warning dream before Caesar is assassinated, Juliet's nightmare of the Capulet's tomb, and the Duke of Clarence's nightmare of death by drowning before he is thrown by Richard III's hired assassins into the butt of malmsey. They can recapitulate the guilty or painful events that have gone before, as Lady Macbeth does while sleepwalking. They may anticipate a disturbing event which is then reversed, as in Henry IV's dream that his son Hal steals his crown. Sometimes it is difficult to distinguish whether certain appearances are ghosts or dreams. The figures that appear in the epilogue to *Saint Joan* are dreams, but are embodied and function as ghosts, as do the appearances that torment Richard III and Brutus.

The notion of the entire dramatic world as being itself a dream is suggested in the titles of a number of plays—*A Midsummer Night's Dream, The Dream Play, Life's a Dream, An American Dream*. The dreams of the three main characters in *Frank Miller* were focused toward the future—the ideal world for which each of them longed. These utopian visions provided an ironic commentary on and a powerful contrast with the harsh truth of the real situation in which they found themselves. In *Famous People* and *The Seal Wife,* the dreams of the protagonists recalled past moments of intense love or loss, success or failure, and showed the contrasting nature of the worlds between which they were torn.

One of the most significant reasons for including a dream in a dramatic sequence is that it allows, and indeed encourages, an escape from naturalism. Words, actions, and sounds in a dream can be patterned and distorted in a grotesque but highly significant manner. The dream also provides a strong temporal orientation—a reliving of a happy or painful past incident or a premonition of future happenings.

Madness

Another kind of appearance used frequently by dramatists is that of madness, and in particular an assumed or temporary insanity. Insanity provides a richly ironic commentary on the whole theatre event. The theatre audience has paid to both hear and see unrealities, which it accepts as temporarily genuine. A fantasy is commenting on a fantasy. The madness or fantastic behavior of some characters in a play may serve to authenticate the sanity and sincerity of others—for example, the tormented Duchess of Malfi surrounded by "the convocation of madmen"—or it calls that very sincerity into question as when the "mad" Hamlet is shown in contrast to the duplicity of Claudius, Gertrude, and Polonious. Madness provides a kind of protection for Hamlet, Edgar disguised as Poor Tom, and Pirandello's Henry IV. Lunacy can be seen as another kind of role capable of hiding a "true" identity, or revealing it.

In a process drama using Poe's *The Tell-Tale Heart* as a pre-text, ninth grade students became psychiatrists who had been hired by the protagonist's defense lawyer (the teacher in role) to prove him insane. This man insists on his sanity, but has written a document in which he confesses to the murder but which also may help to save his life. The students in role as psychiatrists examined this statement (the actual story) for clues as to the delusions, obsessions, and paranoia from which he was clearly suffering. They also created tableaux of the key incidents in the story and interviewed neighbors, witnesses, police, and friends and relations of the murderer and the victim. The dramatic world they created was constrained by the text, but went beyond it, as they elaborated on the state of mind of the protagonist. Their knowledge and understanding of the original text was also greatly enhanced.

Rituals

A valuable device for the playwright is the use of rituals and ceremonies. Plays contain processions, feasts, balls, pageants, trials, tournaments, funerals, elections, and coronations. Comedies, including those of Shakespeare, often end with a wedding or some other celebration. Tragedies may include solemn processions, banquets, trials of strength, and funerals, as well as such strangely tender and "maimed" rites as Bosola's ritual preparation of the Duchess of Malfi for her assassination at his hands. The ceremonial, dignified, and celebratory nature of this event contrasts with the almost accidental and absurd deaths of her brothers, the "mad Duke" and the Cardinal, dying "like a leveret." Even Othello's murder of Desdemona has a somber and ritualistic quality.

Ritual is a way of understanding and celebrating our own lives in the context of our communities. In theatre, ritual has the same purpose. Most rituals, although they do not have a plot, embody some kind of significant alteration in those involved, and these changes accompany the turning points of personal and social life—marriage, maturity, change of status, death. In theatre, when ceremonies and rituals are completed, they bring a sense of harmony and fulfillment, as in Rosalind's ritual pairing-off of the lovers at the end of *As You Like It*. Uncompleted or interrupted festivities, rituals, and ceremonies produce the opposite effect. Macbeth's "admired disorder" breaks up the banquet, the news of the king's death interrupts the festivities in *Love's Labour's Lost,* Ophelia's funeral ends in the undignified brawling of Hamlet and Laertes, and Lady Anne's mourning is disturbed by Richard III's unseemly but eventually successful advances. Even in comedy and farce, interrupted or corrupted ceremonies often occur. The refusal of Claudio to marry Hero in *Much Ado About Nothing* almost tips the play toward tragedy. All of these kinds of ritual and ceremony can be included in process drama. They serve to strengthen the sense of patterned action, and provide an important part of the social context of the imagined world.

It is interesting to reflect on the ways in which meals feature in both theatre and process drama. The quarrel over the breakfast table is almost a cliché of the kind of brief improvisation that was often asked of students in drama classes. In theatre, the meal can provide a social action and setting that may be either formal or casual, naturalistic or highly stylized. It holds the characters together in a kind of community that they may celebrate, corrupt, criticize, or destroy. It provides a social frame in which they may and often must continue to encounter each other. In a recent production of Richard III in London's Royal National Theatre, the quarrel between Richard and the other factions surrounding the dying King Edward took place at a formal dinner table. The contrast between the elegance of the setting and the naked aggression and jostling for power of the characters was very striking.

The earlier in the day a theatrical meal occurs, the less formal and more naturalistic it is likely to be. Of course, this reflects the position of these occasions in the real world, where breakfast is the most casual meal of the day, unless it is the "levee" of an important personage. Examples of meals in varying degrees of formality abound in playwrights as diverse as Marlowe, Shakespeare, Chekhov, Ibsen, Wilder, Coward, Wilde, and Pinter. In *The Long Christmas Dinner,* Wilder constructed an entire play and the history of a family over several generations by containing the events within an endless family celebration.

Each of these occasions can be seen as a reflection on the social context in which it is set, and it often provides an ironic commentary on that context. It is possible to use the social occasion that includes a meal as a part of a process drama and allow the activities and rituals that arise to structure the episode. The disrupted meal to which Frank Miller is invited is a vain attempt to contain this outsider in conventional family life. The struggles of the family to maintain ordinary social behavior allow the tensions within this apparently most mundane situation to accumulate and eventually explode. It is significant that the meal or feast, from the birthday party or Christmas dinner to the wedding breakfast or formal banquet, is one of the few widely accessible social ceremonies left in our society.

A ritual can be used as a pre-text for process drama. I asked highschool students to work in groups and create a tableau of the perfect wedding. Their familiarity with this ritual occasion gave them the freedom to be both playful and ironic. All individuals in each group wrote a single thought on a scrap of paper, a thought they would not want to speak publicly. Then each group exchanged their writing at random with another group. The result was that the banality of the perfect wedding was subverted by the random quality of this text. The students labored to make meaning from what became a kind of subtext, and went on to develop the theme in further episodes.

In an attempt to revitalize the stage, Artaud called for a return to a ritualized theatre, which would include music, rhythmical movements, masks, effigies, light, and color. Attempts by avant-garde ensembles to follow Artaud and re-create or concoct ritual events may result in experiences that are both disturbing and disorienting. In real life and in theatre, ritual has a complex function, including the significant one of distancing and containing emotion. It can be seen not merely as a repetition of the event it celebrates or refers to, but also as a properly distanced *recurrence*. This makes its inclusion in process drama valuable both structurally and emotionally.

Music, Dance, and Song

The placing of music and dance within a dramatic sequence can prove very effective. Music emphasizes or defamiliarizes a mood or situation, as in the sounds of Prospero's isle or *Twelfth Night*. It also has a significant ritual function and accompanies ceremonies and masques. Songs can be vehicles for ironic commentary, counterpoint, emotional relief, and reflection. Both Shakespeare and Brecht use songs to comment on characters and situations, for example, in *As You Like It* and *Mother Courage,* as well as for narrative purposes, and to mislead and misinform, as in Ariel's song "Full Fathom Five" in *The Tempest.* They can even be battles of wit and will between the protagonists, as in Pinter's *Old Times* and between Jacques and the forest lords in *As You Like It.*

Many plays include dances that have a precise dramatic and structural function, emphasizing a theme or a highly charged moment, for example, the dances in *Love's Labour's Lost* or Nora's tarantella in *The Doll's House*. I have already mentioned the effectiveness of the dances in *Dancing at Lughnasa*. In *Lady Betty*, an interesting play by the innovative British director Declan Donnellan, an Irish step dance became a contest between two of the characters. The folkdance at the end of the process drama *The Seal Wife* had a ceremonial, celebratory, and reflective quality.

Public and Private Dimensions

Rituals and ceremonies provide useful occasions for major public encounters in both theatre and process drama. In one sense, all drama is public, because it is spectacular by nature, a shared and manifest creation. But the contrast between the kind of scene that has a deliberately public dimension—Macbeth's banquet, or the very public discovery of Duncan's murder, and the secrecy, privacy, and intimacy of the scenes between the Macbeths—is very striking. The involuntary public quality of intensely private occasions can also be effective, for example, Lady Macbeth's sleepwalking scene, in which the privacy of her very soul becomes public property.

Improvised drama may too often rely on the creation of scenes that are essentially private, and fail to contrast and contextualize these private and domestic moments with scenes where a sense of the concerns of the community and the broader social setting can be established. Meetings, conferences, inquiries, ceremonies, public declarations, trials, and funerals are all useful and revealing public occasions that can be woven into the unfolding text of the dramatic world. These large group events contrast strongly with the private encounters between two characters, as the original meeting of townsfolk in *Frank Miller* contrasts with Frank's meeting with his son. The public nature of the first scene does not necessarily mean that there is greater honesty or disclosure. In both, things long hidden lurk beneath the surface of the interaction. *Famous People* usefully contrasts the public demands and private needs of the participants.

Conclusion

A recognition of the power and potential of highlighting dramatic and structural devices in process drama has grown in recent years among teachers of drama. Unfortunately, there is little indication that a similar understanding of the potential of these developments exists among those who are training actors or using improvisation in theatre. There seem to be few theorists and practitioners of improvisation in theatre who understand that its structure can go beyond mechanical decisions about who, what, and where, that the audience can be integrated into the event, and that this structure can clearly reveal the workings of dramatic form.

Knowledge of dramatic structure and its workings within process drama will not necessarily ensure a truly creative and organic process, but it may prevent our abandoning our efforts when the challenges presented by this way of working seem too daunting or when we face pressures from outside forces to turn our process into product. Every genuinely artistic mode of expression involves taking risks and stepping into the unknown. However much we know about the process, it can never be reduced to a set of formulae, and, if it is truly improvisatory, it will always take us by surprise. The drama process can be used instrumentally to accomplish specific purposes, but finally it is its own destination. The experience is its own reward.

Although process drama is essentially improvised, it is not a matter of casting off all forms and limitations in order to be free and spontaneous. We use these forms and constraints in order to transcend them. The solution is to create a dramatic moment that is so intriguing and tantalizing that it inevitably leads us on to the next moment. Each moment begins to grow and evolve its own structure, its own imagined world, with its own identity. It acquires a momentum that develops in accordance with the rules guiding the unfolding of any dramatic world.

In this drama world, participants are free to alter their status, adopt different roles and responsibilities, play with elements of reality, and explore alternate existences. When the drama world takes hold and acquires a life of its own, all of the participants will return across the threshold of that world changed in some way, or at least not quite the same as when they began. The key to both the power and the purpose of process drama and theatre lies in the fact that they not only permit but also demand that we discover other versions of ourselves in the roles we play or watch other actors playing. We slip the bonds of our identities and participate in other forms of existence.

At their most powerful, neither theatre nor process drama has as definable or detachable a thing as a message or even a precise "learning area." One can't, for example, say that *Hamlet* is about revenge or *Othello* about jealousy. This is not what these great texts teach us. Instead, they create an experience of intensity and significance from which we emerge changed in some way. Both theatre and process drama operate what Boal calls a "politics of the imagination." They give us a vision of our humanity and a sense of the possibilities facing us and the society in which we live. Reflection and distance, both key concepts in successful drama, are crucial elements in achieving a sense of alternatives.

Other art forms offer us new worlds, worlds in which we can feel but not act, worlds for contemplation. In process drama, we go beyond that. We create the world and live, however briefly, by its laws. When we return from these alternate worlds to our own realities, we are likely to bring a kind of dissatisfaction with us, a degree of alienation. This is not merely escapism or frustration, but also a necessary consequence of imagination. To imagine something, we must transcend the boundaries of reality. We must be unwilling to let things stay as they are, to be at home with our realities. Both imagination and dissatisfaction are preconditions for positive change. If we cannot imagine things differently, we will not be able to bring about any alteration in our circumstances.

As theatre and process drama share structure and form, so too they share a purpose. Drama, whether scripted, devised, or improvised, is a way of thinking about life. The characters, situations, events, and issues that are created and explored within the dramatic world reflect and illuminate the real world. If drama is a mirror, its purpose is not merely to provide a flattering reflection that confirms our existing understanding. It must be used as mirrors often are, as a means of seeing ourselves more clearly and allowing us to begin to correct whatever is amiss. It is not merely an instrument of reference, but also a place of disclosure. Drama is an art form that generates and embodies significant meanings and raises significant questions. Every dramatic act is an act of discovery and our acknowledgement of our humanity and community, first in the drama world and then in the real world.

Notes

Introduction

1. O'Neill, C. and A. Lambert. 1982. *Drama Structures: A Practical Handbook for Teachers*. London: Hutchinson. The structures described in this book owe much to the work of both Dorothy Heathcote and Gavin Bolton. In particular, Bolton's *Towards a Theory of Drama in Education* provides the basis for determining the choice of episodes within each structure.
2. O'Toole, J. 1992. *The Process of Drama: Negotiating Art and Meaning*. London: Routledge, p. 2.
3. Bolton, G. 1979. *Towards a Theory of Drama in Education*. London: Longman.
4. Johnson, L. and C. O'Neill. 1984. *Dorothy Heathcote: Collected Writings on Education and Drama*. London: Hutchinson.
5. Lacey, S. and B. Woolland. 1992. "Educational Drama And Radical Theatre Practice." *New Theatre Quarterly* 8 (29); p. 85.
6. Haseman, B. 1991. "Improvisation, Process Drama and Dramatic Art." *The Drama Magazine* (July): p. 20.

Chapter 1

1. Borland, H. 1963. *When the Legends Die*. New York: Lippincott.
2. See Rogers, T. and C. O'Neill. 1993. "Creating Multiple Worlds: Drama, Language and Literary Response" in *Exploring Texts: The Role of Discussion and Writing in the Teaching and Learning of Literature*. Edited by G.E. Newell and R.K. Durst. Norwood, MA: Christopher-Gordon Publishers.
3. Stanislavski, C. 1967. *An Actor Prepares*. London: Penguin Books, p. 54.
4. Stanislavski, C. 1968. *Building a Character*. London: Eyre Methuen, p. 72.
5. Banu, G. 1987. "Peter Brook's Six Days." *New Theatre Quarterly* 3 (10) p. 103.

6. Brook, P. 1972. *The Empty Space.* London: Penguin Books, p. 126.
7. Goorney, H. 1981. *The Theatre Workshop Story.* London: Eyre Methuen.
8. Marowitz, C. 1978. *The Act of Being.* London: Secker and Warburg, p. 58.

Chapter 2

1. Rivers, J. 1987. *Enter Talking.* London: W.H. Allen, pp. 269–270.
2. Johnstone, K. 1979. *Impro.* London: Faber and Faber, p. 27. This book is one of the most useful explorations of the nature of improvisation in print. Clive Barker regards Johnstone's approach as the ultimate development of Stanislavski's work, although Johnstone himself claims that he began by consciously reacting against Stanislavski's ideas. (Barker, C. 1989. "Games in Theatre and Education." *New Theatre Quarterly* 5 (19) p. 230.)
3. Nicoll, A. 1962. *The Theatre and Dramatic Theory.* Cambridge: Cambridge University Press, p. 12.
4. Pavis, P. 1982. *Languages of the Stage: Essays in the Semiology of Theatre.* New York: Performing Arts Journal Publications, p. 141.
5. For a fuller account of this drama lesson, see O'Neill, C. and A. Lambert. 1982. *Drama Structures.* London: Hutchinson.
6. Witkin, R.W. 1974. *The Intelligence of Feeling.* London: Heinemann, p. 181.
7. Johnstone, 1979. op. cit..
8. Wilshire, B. 1982. *Role Playing and Identity.* Bloomington: Indiana University Press, p. 89.
9. Wilshire, ibid, p. 21.
10. Brook, P. 1968. *The Empty Space.* London: Penguin, p. 152.
11. Johnstone, K. 1979. op. cit.
12. Schechner, R. 1982. *The End of Humanism.* New York: Performing Arts Journal Publications, p. 33.
13. Program notes for "Three Works," performances by the Wooster Group at the Tramway Theatre in Glasgow, 4–19 October, 1990.
14. Mike Leigh, in an interview with Sarah Hemming, "Casting about for Ideas." *The Independent.* 8 August, 1990, p. 15. The subsequent quotations from Leigh and/or one of his actresses are also from this interview.
15. Bradbrook, M.C. 1965. *English Dramatic Form.* London: Chatto and Windus, p. 198.

Chapter 3

1. Pavis, P. 1992. *Theatre at the Crossroads of Culture.* London: Routledge, p. 49.
2. Grotowski, J. 1969. *Towards a Poor Theatre.* London: Methuen, p. 57.
3. Innes, C. 1981. *Holy Theatre: Ritual and the Avant Garde,* Cambridge: Cambridge University Press, p. 168.
4. O'Toole, J. 1992. *The Process of Drama.* London: Routledge, p. 137.
5. Rosenblatt, L. 1978. *The Reader, the Text, the Poem: The Transactional Theory of the Literary Work.* Carbondale: Southern Illinois Press.
6. Johnson, L. and C. O'Neill. 1984. *Dorothy Heathcote: Collected Writings on Education and Drama.* London: Hutchinson, p. 130. See also O'Toole, J. 1992. op. cit., pp. 32–33,136–140.

7. Langer, S. 1953. *Feeling and Form.* New York: Scribner.
8. Booth, D. 1985. "Imaginary Gardens with Real Toads: Reading and Drama in Education." *Theory into Practice* 24 (3) p. 196.
9. Booth, ibid.
10. Morgan, N. and J. Saxton. 1987. *Teaching Drama.* London: Hutchinson, p. 2. This generally useful and thought-provoking book defines two kinds of focus—the dramatic focus and the teacher's educational focus, which appears to be synonymous with the teacher's aims for the lesson.

    John O'Toole (1992) p. 103. op. cit., discusses the notion of focus at some length and closely associates it with the purposes of the teacher.

Chapter 4

1. Van Laan, T. 1970. *The Idiom of Drama.* Ithaca: Cornell University Press, p. 229.
2. Fergusson, F. 1969. *The Idea of a Theatre.* Cambridge, MA: Harvard University Press, p. 238.
3. Spolin, V. 1963. *Improvisation for the Theatre.* Evanston, IL: Northwestern University Press, p. 382.
4. Beckerman, B. 1990. *Theatrical Presentation: Performer, Audience and Act.* New York: Routledge, p. 147.
5. Johnson, L. and C. O'Neill. 1984. *Dorothy Heathcote: Collected Writings on Education and Drama.* London: Hutchinson, p. 162.
6. Brook, P. 1968. *The Empty Space.* London: Penguin Books, p. 122.
7. Wright, L. 1985. "Preparing Teachers to Put Drama into the Classroom." *Theory into Practice* 14 (3).
8. Bolton, G. 1984. "Teacher in Role and Teacher Power." Unpublished paper.
9. Blatner, A. and A. Blatner. 1988. *The Art of Play.* New York: Human Sciences Press, p. 23. The authors argue for the adult's need to remain playful and spontaneous. They recommend a form of structured improvisation with many similarities to educational drama, therapy, and play.
10. Johnstone, K. 1979. *Impro.* London: Faber and Faber, p. 84. I was fortunate enough to work with Johnstone in the seventies, and watched him model these capacities most effectively. He gave those with whom he worked the courage to risk joining him in daring and imaginative explorations.
11. Bruner, J. 1962. *On Knowing: Essays for the Left Hand.* London: Athenaeum Press, p. 25.
12. Cranston, J.W. 1991. *Transformations through Drama.* Lanham, MD: University Press of America, pp. 220–226. This handbook offers a variety of helpful ideas for teachers, but the "scenario" format may limit real participation or decision making by the participants.
13. Witkin, R.W. 1974. *The Intelligence of Feeling.* London: Heinemann.
14. Dewey, J. 1934. *Art as Experience.* London: Allen and Unwin, p. 138.
15. Schmitt, N.C. 1990. *Actors and Onlookers: Theatre and Twentieth Century Views of Nature.* Evanston, IL: Northwestern University Press, p. 15.
16. McLaren, P. 1988. "The Liminal Servant and the Ritual Roots of Critical Pedagogy." *Language Arts* 65 (2) pp. 164–179. McLaren is very much aware of the power and potential of drama in the curriculum.

17. Turner, V. 1982. *From Ritual to Theatre: The Human Seriousness of Play.* New York: Performing Arts Journal Publications, p. 114. Turner's work has influenced both Schechner and McLaren.
18. Schechner, R. 1988. *Performance Theory.* New York: Routledge, p. 164.
19. Shklovsky, V. 1965. "Art as Technique." In *Russian Formalist Criticism.* Edited by L. Lemon and M. Reis. Lincoln: University of Nebraska Press, p. 4.
20. Brook, op. cit., p. 43.

Chapter 5

1. Pavis, P. 1992. *Theatre at the Crossroads of Culture.* New York: Routledge, p. 10.
2. Barthes. R. 1972. *Critical Essays.* Evanston, IL: Northwestern University Press, p. 49.
3. Barthes, R. Ibid., p. 27.
4. Zola, E. [1881] 1961. "Naturalism on the Stage." in *Playwrights on Playwriting.* Edited by T. Cole. New York: Hill and Wang, p. 6.
5. Strindberg, A. [1888] 1969. "Miss Julie." *Strindberg's One-Act Plays.* Translated by A. Paulson. New York: Washington Square Press.
6. Ricoeur, P. 1985. *Time and Narrative.* Chicago: University of Chicago Press, p. 21.
7. Mann, T. [1908] 1988. "Essay on the Theatre." Cited in Pfister, M. *The Theory and Analysis of Drama.* Cambridge: Cambridge University Press, p. 162.
8. Kerr, W. 1955. *How not to write a play.* New York: Simon and Schuster, p. 104. This enormously witty and practical book by a theatre critic with many years' experience is full of important insights into theatre structure and audience response.
9. Saint-Denis, M. 1960. *Theatre: The Re-Discovery of Style.* New York: Theatre Arts Books, p. 89.
10. Wilder, T. 1962. "Preface" to *Three Plays: Our Town, The Skin of Our Teeth and The Matchmaker.* London: Penguin, p. 11.
11. Burns, E. 1972. *Theatricality: A Study of Convention in the Theatre and in Social Life.* London: Longman, p. 17.
12. Sartre, J.P. 1976. *Sartre on Theatre.* New York: Random House, p. 162.
13. Grotowski, J. 1968. *Towards a Poor Theatre.* London: Methuen, p. 87.
14. Alfreds, M. 1978–79. "A Shared Experience: The Actor as Story-teller." in *Theatre Papers: The Third Series.* Dartington, UK: Dartington College of the Arts, No. 6, p. 4.
15. Wertenbaker, T. 1988. *Our Country's Good.* London: Methuen, p. 32.
16. Wilder, T. [1941] 1961. "Some Thoughts on Playwriting." In *Playwrights on Playwriting.* Edited by T. Cole. New York: Hill and Wang, p. 106.
17. Mamet, D. 1990. *Some Freaks.* London: Faber and Faber, p. 65.
18. Yeats, W.B. [1916] 1961. "Certain Noble Plays of Japan" in *Essays and Introductions.* London: Macmillan, p. 240.
19. Hornby, R. 1986. *Drama, Metadrama and Perception.* Lewisburg, PA: Bucknell University Press.
20. Burns, op. cit., p. 128.
21. Sartre, J.P. 1957. *Being and Nothingness.* London: Methuen, p. 59.

22. Woolf, V. 1965. *Between the Acts*. London: Harcourt, Brace and World.
23. Camus, A. 1955. *The Myth of Sisyphus and Other Essays*. New York: Vintage Books, p. 59.
24. Moreno, J.L. 1959. *Psychodrama, Vol. II: Foundations of Psychotherapy*. Beacon, NJ: Beacon House, p. 140.
25. Johnson, L. and C. O'Neill. 1984. *Dorothy Heathcote: Collected Writings on Education and Drama*. London: Hutchinson, p. 51.
26. O'Toole, J. 1992. *The Process of Drama*. London: Routledge, p. 86.
27. Bolton, G. 1984. *Drama as Education*. London: Longman, pp. 123–124.
28. Johnson, L. and C. O'Neill. 1984. op. cit., p. 129.
29. Bolton, G. 1988. "Drama as Art." *Drama Broadsheet* 5 (3).
30. Morgan, N. and J. Saxton. 1986. *Teaching Drama*. London: Hutchinson, p. 30.
31. Bolton, 1988, op. cit., p. 18.
32. Increasingly, writers on theatre form have recognized the significance of roleplaying within the role as both a structural device and a motivating force. A very thorough study of roleplaying in Shakespeare is that by Van Laan, 1978. *Role-playing in Shakespeare*. (Toronto: University of Toronto Press.) There is an illuminating chapter on roleplaying within the role in Hornby, 1986. op. cit.
33. It is worth noting that even in *The Farmer and the Hooker* improvisation from Second City, where the hooker turns out to be a rugmaker, the effectiveness of the interaction and the joke lies in the misunderstanding between the protagonists and the essential denial of role.
34. Barthes, 1972. op. cit., p. 27.
35. George, D.E.R. 1989. "Quantum Theatre—Potential Theatre: A New Paradigm." *New Theatre Quarterly* 5 (18) p. 196.
36. Brook, P. 1987. *The Shifting Point*. New York: Harper and Row, p. 66.
37. Bradbrook, M.C. 1965. *English Dramatic Form*. London: Chatto and Windus, p. 13.

Chapter 6

1. Langer, S. 1953. *Feeling and Form*. New York: Scribners, p. 306. Langer's masterly chapter "The Dramatic Illusion" is full of insight into such significant topics for the present study as time, tension, and audience response.
2. Jenkins, I. 1957. "The Aesthetic Object." *The Review of Metaphysics*, 11. (September) p. 10. This insight seems to go some way toward reconciling the arguments about 'universals' and 'particulars' that continue among drama theorists and practitioners.
3. *Aristotle's Poetics*. 1961. Translated by S.H. Butcher. New York: Hill and Wang, Book vii, 5.
4. Wilshire, B. 1982. *Role Playing and Identity: The Limits of Theatrical Metaphor*. Bloomington: University of Indiana Press, p. 22.
5. From an interview with Eugene O'Neill in the New York *Herald Tribune*, November 16, 1924.
6. Johnstone, K. 1979. *Impro*. London: Faber and Faber, p. 142.
7. Fay, W.G. and C. Carswell. 1936. *The Fays of the Abbey*. New York: Harcourt, Brace and Co., p. 166.

8. Szondi, P. 1987. *The Theory of the Modern Drama.* Translated by M.
    Hays. Minneapolis: University of Minnesota Press, p. 91.
9. Williams, T. [1950] 1965. Preface to *The Rose Tattoo* in *European Theories
    of the Drama,* edited by B.H.Clark. New York: Crown Publishers, p. 528.
10. Marranca, B. 1977. *The Theatre of Images.* New York: Drama Book Spe-
    cialists.
11. Langer, op. cit.., p. 307.
12. The entirely improvised show, 'Come Together' was performed at the
    Royal Court Theatre on October 24 and 25, 1970. I was present at this
    highly successful promenade event.
13. States, B.O. 1978. *The Shape of Paradox: An essay on Waiting for Godot.*
    Berkeley: University of California Press, p. 35.
14. Martin Esslin has persuaded us to accept the truth of this popular anecdote.
15. Dewey, J. 1934. *Art as Experience.* London: George Allen and Unwin, p. 155.
16. Johnstone, op. cit.., p. 116.
17. Nachmanovitch, S. 1990. *Free Play: Improvisation in Life and Art.* Los
    Angeles: Jeremy P. Tarcher, p. 18.
18. Burns, E. 1972. *Theatricality: A Study of Convention in the Theatre and in
    Social Life.* London: Longman, p. 96.

Chapter 7

1. Sarcey, F. 1957. "A Theory of the Theatre," in *Papers on Playmaking.* Ed-
    ited by Brander Matthews. New York: Hill and Wang, p. 122.
2. Pavis, P. 1982. *Languages of the Stage: Essays in the Semiology of Theatre.*
    New York: Performing Arts Journal Publications, p. 91.
3. Ibid., p. 77.
4. Barthes, R. 1977. "Diderot, Brecht, Eisenstein." In *Image, Music, Text.*
    London: Fontana, p. 69. Barthes explores this notion by making fascinat-
    ing links between geometry and theatre.
5. Bullough, E. 1937. *Aesthetics: Lectures and Essays.* London: Bowes and
    Bowes, p. 113. This classic essay has been the basis for most subsequent
    discussions of distance.
6. Quigley, A.E. 1985. *The Modern Stage and Other Worlds.* New York:
    Methuen, p. 23.
7. Cole, D. 1975. *The Theatrical Event: A Mythos, a Vocabulary, a Perspec-
    tive.* Middletown, CT: Wesleyan University Press, p.79.
8. Pavis, op. cit.., p. 73.
9. Callow, S. 1984. *Being an Actor.* London: Methuen, p. 73.
10. Wesker, A. 1972."From a Writer's Notebook." *New Theatre Quarterly* 2 (8).
11. Bolton, G. 1979. *Towards a Theory of Drama in Education.* London:
    Longman, p. 93.
12. McGregor, L., K. Robinson and M. Tate. 1977. *Learning through Drama.*
    London: Heinemann, p. 17.
13. Boal, A. 1979. *Theatre of the Oppressed.* London: Pluto Press. Boal's com-
    pany originally performed propaganda plays to those they identified as
    'the oppressed'—peasants, factory workers, women, blacks. They moved
    on to presenting scenes that dramatized an "oppression," halted the action
    at a moment of crisis, and asked their audience for ideas on possible solu-

tions to the problem. Soon Boal realized they could go beyond merely accepting ideas from the audience and including them in the play. Volunteers were invited to try out their alternative ideas and solutions on stage.

14. Boal, A. 1990. "The Cop in the Head: Three Hypotheses." *The Drama Review* 34 (3) p. 38.

15. Bolton, G. 1983. "The Activity of Dramatic Playing." In *Issues in Educational Drama*. Edited by C. Day and J. Norman. Lewes: Falmer Press, p. 54. For Bolton, the psychology of dramatic behavior is of a different order from direct experiencing. There is both submission to the event, and an enhanced degree of detachment.

16. Foreman, R. 1976. *Plays and Manifestos*. New York: New York University Press, p.143. Foreman insists on an active committed stance from his audiences. His aim is not to induce a "wow" reaction, but one that brings the audience into awareness of themselves as an audience.

17. Nachmanovitch, S. 1990. *Free Play: Improvisation in Life and Art*. Los Angeles: Jeremy P. Tarcher, p. 4. The author is a musician who believes strongly in the significance of improvisation and offers interesting insights on play and creativity.

18. Barthes, R. op. cit., p. 72. Barthes compares stage tableaux to the work of Eisenstein in the cinema, where "the film is a contiguity of episodes . . . by vocation anthological."

19. Marranca, B. 1977. *The Theatre of Images*. New York: Drama Book Specialists, p. xii.

20. Schoenberg, A. [1933] 1950. "Brahms the Progressive." in *Style and Idea*. Berkeley: University of California Press, p. 36.

21. Brook, P. 1972. *The Empty Space*. London: Penguin Books, p. 96.

22. Foreman, op. cit.., p. 143.

Chapter 8

1. O'Neill, C. and A. Lambert. 1984. *Drama Structures*. London: Hutchinson, p. 213.

2. All of these examples are from *Drama Structures*.

3. Miller, A. [1958] 1961. *Playwrights on Playwriting*. Edited by T. Cole. New York: Hill and Wang.

Bibliography

Alfreds, A. 1979–80. "A Shared Experience: The Actor as Story-teller." In *Theatre Papers: The Third Series*. Dartington, UK: Dartington College of the Arts, No. 6.

Aristotle's Poetics. 1961. Translated by S.H.Butcher. New York: Hill and Wang.

Artaud, A. 1970. *The Theatre and Its Double*. London: Calder and Boyers.

Banu, G. 1987. "Peter Brook's Six Days." *New Theatre Quarterly* 3 (10).

Barba, E. 1986. *Beyond the Floating Islands*. New York: PAJ Publications.

Barthes, R. 1982. *Critical Essays*. Evanston, IL: Northwestern University Press.

Barthes, R. 1977. *Image, Music, Text*. London: Fontana.

Beckerman, B. 1979. *Dynamics of Drama: Theory and Method of Analysis*. New York: Drama Book Specialists.

Beckerman, B. 1990. *Theatrical Presentation: Performer, Audience and Act*. New York: Routledge.

Blatner, A and A. Blatner. 1988. *The Art of Play: An Adult's Guide to Reclaiming Imagination and Spontaneity*. New York: Human Sciences Press.

Boal, A. 1979. *Theater of the Oppressed*. London: Pluto Press.

Boal, A. 1990. "The Cop in the Head: Three Hypotheses." *The Drama Review* 34 (3).

Bolton, G. 1984. *Drama as Education*. London: Longman.

Bolton, G. 1988. "Drama as Art." *Drama Broadsheet* 5 (3).

Bolton, G. 1979. *Towards a Theory of Drama in Education*. London: Longman.

Bolton, G. 1986. "The Activity of Dramatic Playing." In *Gavin Bolton: Selected Writings on Drama in Education*. edited by D. Davis and C. Lawrence. London: Longman.

Bolton, G. 1984. "Teacher in Role and Teacher Power." Unpublished paper.

Booth, D. 1985. "Imaginary Gardens with Real Toads." *Theory into Practice* 24 (3).

Borland, H. 1963. *When the Legends Die*. New York: Lippincott.

Bradbrook, M.C. 1965. *English Dramatic Form*. London: Chatto and Windus.

Brook, P. 1968. *The Empty Space*. London: Penguin Books.

Brook, P. 1987. *The Shifting Point*. New York: Harper and Row.

Bruner, J. 1962. *On Knowing: Essays for the Left Hand*. London: Atheneum Press.

Bullough, E. 1957. *Aesthetics: Lectures and Essays*. London: Bowes and Bowes.

Burns, E. 1972. *Theatricality: A Study of Convention in the Theatre and in Social Life*. London: Longman.

Callow, C. 1984. *Being an Actor*. London: Methuen.

Camus, A. 1955. *The Myth of Sisyphus and Other Essays*. New York: Vintage Books.

Clements, P. 1983. *The Improvised Play: The Work of Mike Leigh*. London: Methuen.

Cole, D. 1975. *The Theatrical Event*. Middletown, CT: Wesleyan University Press.

Cole, T. 1960. *Playwrights on Playwriting.* New York: Hill and Wang.

Cranston, J.W. 1991. *Transformations through Drama.* Lanham, MD: University Press of America.

Dewey, J. 1934. *Art as Experience.* London: George Allen and Unwin.

Elam, K. 1980. *The Semiotics of Theatre and Drama.* London: Methuen.

Fay, W.G. and C. Carswell. 1936. *The Fays of the Abbey.* New York: Harcourt, Brace and Co.

Fergusson, F. 1969. *The Idea of a Theatre.* Cambridge, MA: Harvard University Press.

Foreman, R. 1976. *Plays and Manifestos.* New York: New York University Press.

Frost, A. and R. Yarrow, 1990. *Improvisation in Drama.* Basingstoke, UK: Macmillan.

George, D.E.R. 1989. "Quantum Theatre—Potential Theatre: A New Paradigm." *New Theatre Quarterly* 5 (18) p. 196.

George, K. 1980. *Rhythm in Drama.* Pittsburgh: University of Pittsburgh Press.

Goorney, H. 1981. *The Theatre Workshop Story.* London: Eyre Methuen.

Grotowski, J. 1969. *Towards a Poor Theatre.* London: Eyre Methuen.

Haseman, B. 1991. "Improvisation, Process Drama and Dramatic Art." *The Drama Magazine* (July).

Heathcote, D. and G. Bolton. 1995. *Drama for Learning: Dorothy Heathcote's Mantle of the Expert Approach to Education.* Portsmouth, NH: Heinemann.

Hilton, J. 1987. *Performance.* London: Macmillan.

Hornby, R. 1986. *Drama, Metadrama and Perception.* Lewisburg, PA: Bucknell University Press.

Innes, C. 1981. *Holy Theatre: Ritual and the Avant Garde.* Cambridge: Cambridge University Press.

Jenkins, I. 1957. "The Aesthetic Object." *The Review of Physics* 11 (September).

Johnson, L. and C. O'Neill. 1984. *Dorothy Heathcote: Collected Writings on Education and Drama.* London: Hutchinson.

Johnstone, K. 1979. *Impro.* London: Faber and Faber.

Kerr, W. 1955. *How Not to Write a Play.* New York: Simon and Schuster.

Kirby, M. 1987. *Formalist Theatre.* Philadelphia: University of Pennslyvania Press.

Kumiega, J. 1978. "Laboratory Theatre/Growtowski/The Mountain Project." In *Theatre Papers: The Second Series.* Dartington, UK: Dartington College of Arts, 9.

Lacey, S. and B. Woolland. 1992. "Educational Drama and Radical Theatre Practice." *New Theatre Quarterly* 8 (29).

Langer, S. 1953. *Feeling and Form.* New York: Scribner.

Mamet, D. 1989. *Some Freaks.* London: Faber and Faber.

Mamet, D. 1986. *Writing in Restaurants.* London: Faber and Faber.

Marowitz, C. 1978. *The Act of Being.* London: Secker and Warburg.

Marranca, B. 1977. *The Theatre of Images.* New York: Drama Book Specialists.

Matthews, B. 1957. *Papers on Playmaking.* New York: Hill and Wang.

McLaren, P. 1988. "The Liminal Servant and the Ritual Roots of Critical Pedagogy." *Language Arts* 65 (2).

McGregor, L., K. Robinson and M. Tate. 1977. *Learning through Drama.* London: Heinemann.

Moreno, J.L. 1959. *Psychodrama: Volume II: Foundations of Psychotherapy.* Beacon, NJ: Beacon House.

Morgan, N. and J. Saxton. 1986. *Teaching Drama.* London: Hutchinson.

Nachmanovich, S. 1990. *Free Play: Improvisation in Life and Art.* Los Angeles: Jeremy P. Tarcher, Inc.

Nicoll, A. 1962. *The Theatre and Dramatic Theory.* London: Harrap.

O'Neill, C. 1978. "Drama and the Web of Form." Unpublished M.A. dissertation, Durham University.

O'Neill, C., A. Lambert, R. Linnell, and J. Warr-Wood. 1977. *Drama Guidelines.* London: Heinemann.

O'Neill, C., and A. Lambert. 1982. *Drama Structures.* London: Hutchinson.

O'Toole, J. 1992. *The Process of Drama: Negotiating Art and Meaning.* London: Routledge.

Pavis, P. 1982. *Languages of the Stage: Essays in the Semiology of the Theatre.* New York: Performing Arts Journal Publications.

Pavis, P. 1992. *Theatre at the Crossroads of Culture.* London: Routledge.

Quigley, A. 1985. *The Modern Stage and Other Worlds.* New York: Methuen.

Ricoeur, P. 1985. *Time and Narrative.* Chicago: University of Chicago Press.

Rivers, J. 1987. *Enter Talking.* London: W.H. Allen.

Robinson, K. 1980. *Exploring Theatre and Drama.* London: Heinemann.

Rogers, T. and C. O'Neill. 1993. "Creating Multiple Worlds: Drama, Language and Literary Response" in *Exploring Texts: The Role of Discussion and Writing in the Teaching and Learning of Literature.* Edited by G. Newell and R.K. Durst. Norwood, MA: Christopher-Gordon Publishers.

Roose-Evans, J. 1984. *Experimental Theatre.* London: Routledge and Kegan Paul.

Rosenblatt, L. 1978. *The Reader, the Text, the Poem: The Transactional Theory of the Literary Work.* Carbondale: Southern Illinois Press.

Saint-Denis, M. 1960. *The Re-discovery of Style.* New York: Theatre Arts Books.

Sarcey, F. 1957. "A Theory of the Theatre," in *Papers on Playmaking.* Edited by B. Matthews. New York: Hill and Wang.

Sartre, J.P. 1957. *Being and Nothingness.* London: Methuen.

Sartre, J.P. 1976. *Sartre on Theatre.* New York: Pantheon Books.

Schechner, R. 1988. *Performance Theory.* New York: Routledge.

Schechner, R. 1969. *Public Domain: Essays on the Theatre.* New York: Bobs-Merrill.

Schechner, R. 1982. *The End of Humanism.* New York: Performing Arts Journal Publications.

Schmitt, N. C. 1990. *Actors and Onlookers: Theatre and Twentieth Century Views of Nature.* Evanston, IL: Northwestern University Press.

Sheldon, S. 1969. *Theatre Double Game.* Charlotte: University of North Carolina Press.

Shklovsky, V. 1965. "Art as Technique." In *Russian Formalist Criticism.* Edited by L. Lemon and M. Reis. University of Nebraska Press.

Spolin, V. 1962. *Improvisation for the Theatre.* Evanston, IL: Northwestern University Press.

Stanislavski, C. 1969. *An Actor Prepares.* London: Geoffrey Bles.

Stanislavski, C. 1968. *Building a Character.* London: Eyre Methuen.

States, B.O. 1987. *Great Reckonings in Little Rooms: On the Phenomenology of Theater.* Berkeley: University of California Press.

States, B.O. 1971. *Irony and Drama.* Ithaca: Cornell University Press.

States, B.O. 1978. *The Shape of Paradox.* Berkeley: University of California Press.

Stein, G. 1975. "Plays" in *Lectures in America.* New York: Vintage Books.

Strindberg, A. [1888] 1969. "Miss Julie." *Strindberg's One-Act Plays.* Translated by A. Paulson. New York: Washington Square Press.

Szondi, P. 1987. *The Theory of the Modern Drama*. Translated by M. Hays. Minne-apolis: University of Minnesota Press.

Turner, V. 1982. *From Ritual to Theatre: The Human Seriousness of Play*. New York: PAJ Publications.

Van Laan, T. 1970. *The Idiom of Drama*. Ithaca: Cornell University Press.

Van Laan, T. 1978. *Role Playing in Shakespeare*. Toronto: University of Toronto Press.

Wagner, B.J. 1976. *Dorothy Heathcote: Dramas as a Learning Medium*. Washington, D.C.: National Education Association.

Watson, I. 1989. "Eugenio Barba: The Latin American Connection." *New Theatre Quarterly* 5 (17).

Wesker, Arnold. 1972. "From a Writer's Notebook." *New Theatre Quarterly* 2 (8) p. 8–13.

Wilder, T. 1962. Preface to *Three Plays*. London: Penguin.

Wilder, T. 1960. "Some Thoughts on Playwriting." In *Playwrights on Playwriting*. edited by T. Cole. New York: Hill and Wang.

Wiles, T.J. 1980. *The Theater Event*. Chicago: University of Chicago Press.

Willett, J. 1957. *Brecht on Theatre*. New York: Hill and Wang.

Williams, T. 1965. Preface to *The Rose Tattoo*, 1950. In *European Theories of the Drama*. Edited by Barrett Clark. New York: Crown Publishers.

Wilshire, B. 1982. *Role Playing and Identity: The Limits of Theatre as Metaphor*. Bloomington: Indiana University Press.

Witkin, R.W. 1974. *The Intelligence of Feeling*. London: Heinemann.

Woolf, Virginia. [1941] 1969. *Between the Acts*. New York: Harcourt, Brace and World.

Wright, L. 1985. "Preparing Teachers to Put Drama in the Classroom." *Theory into Practice*. 14 (3) 1985; pp. 205–210.

Yeats, W.B. 1961. *Essays and Introductions*. London: Macmillan.

Zola, E. 1961. "Naturalism on the Stage." In *Playwrights on Playwriting*. Edited by T. Cole. New York: Hill and Wang.

Index

165